investiture in London in February 1986 and the magnificent rôle played by so many uniformed Papal Knights. It was a very special occasion because the Papal Knights had invited the Knights of other Catholic Orders to take part in their formal attire.

It is because of my happy memories of the Papal Knights in Great Britain that I gladly accepted the invitation to write these words, and place on record a few thoughts about the important rôle Papal Knights have to play and what we must expect from the Pontiff's own Knights. Those of us who have been in the service of the Supreme Pontiff — some for over half a century — are proud of our Papal Knights. We welcome, therefore, the fact that after so many years the guidelines for their duties have been worked out, collected and published.

Palazzo di S. Carlo
Città del Vaticano
20 June 1987

+ Jacques Martin

PART I

The chapters in Part I deal exclusively with matters concerning Knights of the Pontifical Equestrian Orders, the Papal Knights.

The Cross on the Sword was originally conceived solely as a volume of guidelines for Papal Knights, but so many legal and procedural matters, and complex problems, had arisen out of the contents of the 1985 edition of *Orders of Knighthood, Awards and the Holy See*, that further parts were added to it. *The Cross on the Sword* is a supplement and should be seen in that context.

Part I has nine chapters: the first two chapters deal with the rôle and function of Papal Knights, the growth of the different Orders and their administration, the privileges granted to Papal Knights, the proposal procedure for a papal knighthood and the administrative work involved in it, up to the Cardinal Secretary of State signing the Papal Brief. Chapter Two also deals with peripheral matters, the insignia, the status of the Orders in the international forum of Orders of Chivalry, the difference between Pontifical Orders of Knighthood and the Catholic Religious Orders of Knighthood, with regard to their standing in the political arena of Chivalry; particular references to privileges granted to Papal Knights by Pope St. Pius X, matters of etiquette and protocol, how to obtain permission from the Head of State to wear the insignia; the present situation concerning the administration of the Pontifical Equestrian Orders and, last but not least, why the juridical position of Papal Knights is different to that of the Knights of all other Orders of Chivalry.

Chapter Three contains the only decress ever promulgated by the Chancellery of the Pontifical Equestrian Orders with regard to uniforms and insignia for the Orders of Pius IX, St. Gregory the Great (civil and military divisions), and the Order of Pope St. Sylvester. A special section draws on the experience of Papal Knights, adding further advice on decorations and the uniform (including travel abroad with the sword, which is looked upon as a dangerous weapon by police, airlines and customs alike).

Chapters Four to Nine give guidelines to Bishops, Parish Priests, Masters of Ceremonies and especially the Knights for services and ceremonies of an investiture. They also deal for the first time with the important question of Pontifical Orders of Knighthood being bestowed on non-Catholics and non-Christians. Two ceremonies, both of which took place in the same Cathedral and in the same archiepiscopal Throne Room, though they were totally different in content and execution, may serve as guidelines for special occasions: one had an investiture as its central part, but was more of a public occasion with television and the press much in evidence. The second was the dignified and moving concelebrated Eucharist by many priests on the occasion of the creation of Sir Harold Hood, Bt., T.D., as a Knight Grand Cross of the Order of St. Gregory the Great after serving as Chairman of the Association of Papal Knights in Great Britain for twenty years, and the conferment of the insignia by the Cardinal Archbishop afterwards in the Throne Room.

At the special request of the Holy See, His Eminence Cardinal Hume of Westminster, Bishop Gerald Mahon of West London, and many parish priests, the chapter dealing with an investiture of Catholic Papal Knights also has a separate section which provides guidelines for a ceremony to be used when conferring the Papal Awards *Pro Ecclesia et Pontifice* and *Benemerenti.*

CHAPTER ONE

THE PONTIFICAL EQUESTRIAN ORDERS

The history of Pontifical Orders of Knighthood and the involvement of the Holy See in the field of Chivalry have been extensively described in *ORDERS OF KNIGHTHOOD, AWARDS AND THE HOLY SEE.* However, it has only been since, and as a result of, the publication of the revised edition that a number of questions have been raised.

Nobody was deliberately withholding information, nor was the reason for the lack of it a breakdown in communication or negligence. Much information was simply not available at the time *ORDERS OF KNIGHTHOOD, AWARDS AND THE HOLY SEE* was written and revised. For example, nobody had enquired about a Grand Chancellor of the Pontifical Equestrian Orders until by comparing them with other Orders of Knighthood, there appeared to be no hierarchical structure or centrally coordinated administration for them. Indeed, the most recently published decrees (which had also been the first) of a Grand Chancellor of the Pontifical Equestrian Orders are dated 7 February 1905.

Only the Pontifical Equestrian Order of St. Gregory the Great had a Grand Chancellor appointed to it in 1831 when Pope Gregory XVI appointed the Secretary of State *pro tempore* to be "Grand Chancellor of this great Order".

There are no precedents for liturgical rites and investitures of Pontifical Knights, and only the ceremonial procedures for Papal Knights which were promulgated by Pope St. Pius X.

For the revised edition of *ORDERS OF KNIGHTHOOD, AWARDS AND THE HOLY SEE* in 1985, His Eminence Agostino Cardinal Casaroli, Secretary of State, allowed his definition of the rôle of a Papal Knight to be published as the prologue. It became the most quoted sentence in the press and media, and it formed the basis for the investiture rites which were compiled in due course. However, I was not aware at the time that Cardinal Casaroli's definition of the rôle of a Papal Knight was the first written statement since February 1905 by the dignitary in whom some of the powers of the former Grand Chancellor of the Pontifical Equestrian Orders had been vested.

Apart from some Papal Briefs of Foundation and Reconstitution of Pontifical Orders, only some Decrees *"EX CANCELLARIA"*, dated 7

February 1905 and signed by Luigi Cardinal Macchi, Grand Chancellor of the Pontifical Equestrian Orders, are the only sources of Information. The latter restrict themselves to describing the uniforms and decorations of the different ranks of the five Equestrian Orders. I shall return to the source material later.

It has always been the tradition of the Holy See to base procedures and ceremonies on precedents unless a specific rule had been promulgated. For the Pontifical Orders of Knighthood there were no precedents which could have been used as guidelines for Papal Knights.

One rule, however, was laid down by Pope St. Pius X and it is of great importance. His Holiness dealt with ceremonial functions and precedence of Pontifical Knights in two ways: he placed the Orders and ranks in clearly defined categories, from the first — the Order of Christ — to the fifth — the Order of Pope St. Sylvester. He also assigned to Papal Knights a ceremonial function by giving them a place in the papal cortège. Many engravings, even those predating the ruling by Pope St. Pius X, show Papal Knights attending upon the Supreme Pontiff, the Cardinals and other high ecclesiastical dignitaries in papal processions.

Some changes in the structure of Pontifical Equestrian Orders were made by Gregory XVI in 1841. 1905 saw the major reconstitution of three of the Pontifical Orders of Knighthood by St. Pius X and changes continued to be made until the middle of the twentieth century.

The Holy See had frowned upon some practices for many decades, and these only ended with Pius XII, who in 1939 — the first year of his pontificate — abolished the titles of nobility which had hitherto been conferred with the ranks of Knight Grand Cross and Knight Commander of the Pian Order which had been founded by Pius IX.

Other procedures, such as dubbing Knights during an investiture, disappeared almost completely after the second World War. However, some procedures and rites of investiture that were based on local traditions, and not on any rulings laid down by the Chancellery of Pontifical Equestrian Orders, seem to have survived in a few countries.

The only Pontifical Order of Knighthood that was given some procedural guidelines for the investiture of its Knights was the Supreme Order of Christ. A medieval religious rite was reproduced in the revised statutes promulgated in 1905 by St. Pius X, but there is no evidence to show that the ceremony was ever used because the Order had been designated for Catholic Monarchs and Heads of State only, and the rite of investiture published for this Order was considered unsuitable for reigning Monarchs and Heads of State.

It is, however, necessary to consider further some aspects of the abolition of titles of nobility conferred with Papal Knighthoods. Many details can be found in *ORDERS OF KNIGHTHOOD, AWARDS AND THE HOLY SEE* and, as is explained on page 22 of that book, Pope Pius XII restricted, if he did not expressly abolish, the bestowal of all titles of nobility. It has been claimed that Pius XII created his nephews princes but this is untrue. It was the King of Italy who bestowed those titles on them. Since the pontificate of Pius XII (1939–1958), successive Pontiffs have more and more reduced the temporal aspects of their exercise of sovereignty.

In the chapter on the Order of the Golden Spur or The Golden Militia (pp. 34–43), it is explained that Pope Gregory XVI had abolished, by Apostolic Brief of 31 October 1841, the title of Count Palatine which the Order had previously conferred.

In spite the firm reiteration of this Apostolic Brief by Pope St. Pius X in 1905, when the Supreme Pontiff re-constituted the Order of the Golden Spur, and frequent reminders in *L'Osservatore Romano*. In 1986, 145 years after the abolition of the titles, I have seen letters with headings and visiting cards from gentlemen who are styled 'Count Palatine' and also use the appellation 'Hereditary Knight of the Golden Spur'.

As far as Pontifical Equestrian Orders are concerned, there have never been hereditary Knighthoods. Until 1841 the Order of the Golden Militia or the Golden Spur had two classes: one which gave to the recipient the title of Count Palatine, which could be inherited by the Knight's sons, (*comes palatinus major*), and another which gave the same title *ad personam*, which ceased to exist after the Knight's death, (*comes palatinus minor*).

Those who are styled Count Palatine, claim inheritance of the title from a *comes palatinus major* of the Order prior to 1841.

Legal questions have been raised from time to time which place claims to the title of a pontifical Count Palatine in some doubt, but the Holy See has never considered the matter important enough to order an official investigation.

The legal objections to the title of Count Palatine being inherited *ad infinitum* are based on the wording of the conferment. Pope Gregory XVI had decreed: "the Knight shall enjoy the title and it can be inherited by his sons"; (*Equites potientur privilegio nobilitatis in filios transmittendae*). Pope Gregory XVI did *not* decree that the title was to be inherited by the heirs in the male line. He used the word *filius* (son) and not the word *heres* (heir) as he had done in other contexts.

Some jurists maintain that the legal position of an inherited papal title of nobility which was conferred with an Order of Knighthood was identical to the appellation "Honourable" which is enjoyed by the sons of British Life Peers. They retain the title after their father's death, but the appellation cannot be inherited by the grandsons of the Life Peers.

The title Count Palatine (which must not be confused with the title of a Count of the Holy Roman Empire), was also attached to several offices at the papal and some royal and ducal courts.

The title 'Knight of the Golden Spur' has never been hereditary, and the Holy See considers such claims fanciful and totally unfounded. Those using the appelation should cease to do so because it is a worthless appellation.

A translation of the Papal Brief, given under the Fisherman's Ring of Pius XII on 11 November 1939, concerning Knights Grand Cross and Knights Commander of the Pian Order, can be found in the chapter on uniforms, after the section on the Pian Knights in this book.

The Pope is Sovereign Head and Grand Master of The Supreme Order of Christ, The Order of the Golden Spur, The Order of Pius IX (or Pian Order), The Order of St. Gregory the Great and the Order of Pope St. Sylvester.

Appointment to all Pontifical Orders of Knighthood is in the personal gift of the Supreme Pontiff. The Orders derive their international recognition from the sovereign status of the Holy See. They are not Orders of the Vatican City State as is so often mistakenly stated: the tri-partite rôle of the Supreme Pontiff and of the Holy See often leads to misunderstandings.

I stated earlier that there appeared to be no hierarchical structure or centrally coordinated administration for the Pontifical Equestrian Orders. This may have been in the mind of Pope John Paul II, when he informed the Secretary of State, who conveyed the message to me, that he was pleased to have this "compendium of facts which hitherto could only be found in scattered and often hard-to-find sources".

These sources are mostly Papal Briefs and an occasional obscure reference to consultations Popes had with certain dignitaries before promulgating a rule or instituting an Order of Knighthood.

On occasion the signatories of Papal Briefs and the titles accorded to them provide clues as to the cardinals who had been given reponsibilities for a Pontifical Equestrian Order and their status in the Roman Curia. When Pope Gregory XVI founded the Order of St. Gregory the Great on 1 September 1831, the Papal Brief instituting the Order was signed in Rome at the Basilica *S. Maria Maggiore* by Cardinal Bernetti, Secretary of State to His Holiness. The Papal Brief of Pope Gregory XVI, dated 30 May 1834, in which he laid down regulations concerning the three classes of Knights in the Order, Knight Grand Cross, Knight Commander and Knight, was signed in Rome at St. Peter's Basilica by A. Picchioni, *Sostituto*, *"per il Signor Card. Albani"*, the Substitute of the Secretariat of State on behalf of Cardinal Albani, the succesor to Cardinal Bernetti as Grand Chancellor.

In the last paragraph, His Holiness appointed as the first Secretary or Grand Chancellor of the Order *"il Cardinale di S. R. Chiesa Segretario dei*

Brevi", the Cardinal Secretary of Briefs of the Holy Roman Church. Pope Gregory charged the Grand Chancellor to ". . . diligently keep a register of the names, ranks, date of admission to the Order and the number of the Knights."

In 1847, Pope Pius IX founded the Pian Order, and the Papal Brief was signed at the Basilica *S. Maria Maggiore* in Rome on 17 June by Cardinal Lambruschini, Secretary of State to His Holiness. Two years later, on 17 June 1849, the Papal Brief concerning the insignia for Pian Knights was signed by Giacomo Cardinal Antonelli *"De speciali mandato SSmi"*, by special mandate of His Holiness. It was signed at Gaeta, where Pope Pius IX had taken refuge since 1848 with King Ferdinand II of the Two Sicilies.

The third Papal Brief, establishing a third class of the Pian Order, was signed by Pope Pius IX personally at the Quirinal Palace in Rome on 11 November 1856. No Secretary or Grand Chancellor of the Pian Order was ever appointed.

On 7 February 1905, Pope St. Pius X undertook a major reform of two Pontifical Equestrian Orders and created a third. The Holy Father issued three Papal Briefs: the first confirmed the Supreme Order of Christ as the highest among the Pontifical Orders of Knighthood; the second reconstituted the Order of the Golden Spur or Golden Militia, and the third instituted the Order of Pope St. Sylvester, giving the Order its separate identity and statutes.

Five almost identical Decrees were also issued *EX CANCELLARIA ORDINUM EQUESTRIUM* — from the Chancellery of the Equestrian Orders. The Orders of Pius IX and of St. Gregory the Great had been retained unchanged, and only the Decree from the Chancellery was added to the Papal Briefs of Gregory XVI and Pius IX.

The statutes of the Supreme Order of Christ contained only the Papal Brief of Pope Pius X, a medieval rite for investing a Knight of that Order, and the Decree from the Chancellery. The statutes of the Order of the Golden Spur consisted of the Papal Brief by St. Pius X reconstituting it as a separate entity from the Order of St. Sylvester, and the Decree from the Chancellery. The Order of Pope St. Sylvester was given the newly promulgated statutes and the Decree from the Chancellery.

The Decrees from the Chancellery are signed by Luigi Cardinal Macchi, *"Magnus Cancellarius Ordinum Equestrium"*, Grand Chancellor of the Pontifical Equestrian Orders. These Decrees refer for the first time to a Chancellery and a Grand Chancellor of all Pontifical Equestrian Orders.

It had been generally assumed that the title used in the Papal Briefs of Gregory XVI and Pius IX, "Cardinal Secretary of Briefs", was the archaic title once used for the Cardinal Secretary of State. However, Secretary of

State of Pope Pius X was Cardinal Rafael Merry del Val, and Cardinal Luigi Macchi was Prefect of the Supreme Tribunal *Signaturae Apostolicae*. The appellation 'Cardinal Secretary of Briefs' appears to have been expressly adopted for those in whom the Supreme Pontiff had vested special responsibilities for a Papal Order of Knighthood, although they were coincidentally Secretaries of State, and finally by Pope St. Pius X for the Grand Chancellor of all the Pontifical Equestrian Orders.

The Decrees *EX CANCELLARIA ORDINUM EQUESTRIUM*, dated 7 February 1905 are the only decrees issued by the Chancellery of the Pontifical Equestrian Orders. Three later Papal Briefs, two by Pius XII, abolishing the titles of nobility previously conferred on Pian Knights (1939), and instituting the Golden Collar of the Pian Order (1957), and one by Paul VI, reserving the Supreme Order of Christ, the Order of the Golden Spur and the Golden Collar of the Pian Knights for Heads of State (1966), were all signed by the Pontiffs themselves.

There is no record of any overt activity of the Chancellery of the Pontifical Equestrian Orders after 1905, and my attempts to obtain answers to the questions I was asked after I had revised Archbishop Cardinale's work, did not meet with much success. I finally wrote to the Cardinal Secretary of State and asked whether His Eminence was by any chance the Grand Chancellor of the Pontifical Equestrian Orders. I also asked if the Chancellery still existed even if in name only. His Eminence and his Secretary, Mons. Luigi Ventura, had soon traced both the Chancellor and the Chancellery — or at least their successors.

On 15 August 1967, Paul VI issued the Constitution *"Regimini Ecclesiae Universae"* in which he decreed that a substantial part of the structure of the Curia was to be changed. Many commissions, secretariats and chancelleries were 'suppressed'.

In the juridical context of Catholic Orders of Knighthood 'suppression' does not imply that an Order has been abolished. Applying the same meaning of the word 'suppression' in the context of the Constitution, Pope Paul VI did not abolish the commissions, secretariats and chancelleries; he reassigned the work which had been done by them to larger departments of the Holy See's administration.

The Chancellery of the Pontifical Equestrian Orders was 'suppressed', but its functions were assigned to the Secretariat of State. The functions of the Grand Chancellor of the Pontifical Equestrian Orders were by implication assigned to the Cardinal Secretary of State. According to the *Annuario Pontificio* the Secretariat of State has a Commission for Pontifical Honours (*Commissione per le Onorificenze*). Those familiar with the annual publication *L'Attività della Santa Sede* may remember that until 1964 this

28

voluminous book carried a substantial section: *"Onorificenze Pontificie"*. The first part gave a list of all ecclesiastical honours the reigning Pope had bestowed in the previous year, such as appointments to *Prelato d'Onore di Sua Santità* or *Cappellano di Sua Santità*. The second part listed all appointments and promotions within the Pontifical Equestrian Orders. At the request of Paul VI subsequent editions of *L'Attività della Santa Sede* only carried the list of ecclesiastical appointments. Appointments and promotions in the Pontifical Equestrian Orders were published in the regular official bulletin of the Holy See, *Acta Apostolicae Sedis*.

.At the end of March 1987 I spent a week in the Vatican, trying to find the members of the Pontifical Honours Commission. Unfortunately, the two Monsignori who had specialised in matters relating to Pontifical Equestrian Orders had died in the last few years, and matters such as processing applications for Papal Knighthoods, the preparation of Papal Briefs and finally the listing of an appointment in the *Acta Apostolicae Sedis* had become more of a collective responsibility of the Secretariat of State; these tasks are carried out by officials of the Secretariat of State who are assigned to that particular function. The Permanent Honours Commission deals with ecclesiastical appointments only.

In his Constitution *Regimini Ecclesiae Universae*, Paul VI had made a further change with regard to the signing of Papal Briefs of Appointment to Pontifical Equestrian Orders by the Secretary of State. Earlier Cardinals holding this position had signed Papal Briefs *de speciali mandato*, holding the special mandate of the Supreme Pontiff to do so. Paul VI decreed that the Secretary of State no longer needed a special mandate when signing Papal Briefs of Appointment in a Pontifical Equestrian Order but could sign *non de mandato*, in his own right as Secretary of State in whom powers of a Grand Chancellor of the Pontifial Equestrian Orders had been vested.

However, Pope Paul also assigned specific tasks which had previously been the responsibility of the Grand Chancellor to other dignitaries in the Secretariat of State.

The Secretary of State *pro tempore* is His Eminence Cardinal Agostino Casaroli, who was appointed to the office in 1979. His Eminence therefore became by implication the Grand Chancellor of the Pontifical Equestrian Orders, though it is a title he does not use. The Constitution *Regimini Ecclesiae Universae* has complicated matters somewhat if one looks for specific Officers of the Papal Orders of Knighthood or tries to obtain counsel on specialised subjects. Besides the sad loss of the two experts, the Constitution is sometimes most generous in assigning tasks to enormous departments such as the Secretariat of State, but also ambiguous when taking into account that, for example, the Secretariat of State carries a

Archbishop Martin and Cardinal Casaroli

"Those of us who are in the service of the Supreme Pontiff are proud of our Papal Knights." Archbishop Jacques Martin, 20-VII-1987.

burden of responsibilities which increases annually by a substantial amount without necessarily any increase in personnel or facilities. Also, in the final analysis, *Regimini Ecclesiae Universae* refers back to the Supreme Pontiff all controversial matters or points in dispute with regard to Pontifical Honours.

It was therefore necessary to research into and clarify such rules and regulations for Papal Knights as had been promulgated by successive Pontiffs, and where necessary interpret them in a contemporary framework.

Pope St. Pius X ratified or newly promulgated the statutes of the Pontifical Orders of Knighthood, and His Holiness defined their juridical status as 'corporations'. This means Papal Knights are a group of individuals belonging to a certain body, but they are not in the strict juridical sense of the term a body corporate, legally authorised to act as a single entity or having the capacity of perpetual succession.

The juridical status of Papal Knights has not changed since St. Pius X defined it. Consequently, the legal status of a national Association of Papal Knights can never be the same as, for example, the juridical status of a National Association of the Sovereign Military Order of Malta or a Lieutenancy of the Equestrian Order of the Holy Sepulchre of Jerusalem. A national Association of Papal Knights has no mandate to speak or act on behalf of the Papal Knights in that country, nor is the Association responsible for acts or statements of individual Papal Knights.

As I explained earlier, St. Pius X assigned to Papal Knights a place in the papal cortège and ceremonial functions. In formulating my interpretation and making the rulings of St. Pius X relevant for today, I was most fortunate to have the benefit of the wise counsel and experience of His Excellency Archbishop Jacques Martin, Prefect of the Pontifical Household from 1964 to the end of 1986, still a Consultant to the Secretariat of State, and the Prelate who has been responsible for protocol and etiquette during state visits by foreign Heads of State and abroad when travelling over half a million kilometres with Popes Paul VI and John Paul II all over the world. In addition, Archbishop Martin has lived in the Vatican for over half a century and served under six Popes.

His Excellency agreed that it was reasonable to assume that Papal Knights throughout the world cannot all take a place in the papal cortège, but that in the Local Churches their place transfers automatically to episcopal cortèges. Consequently, the same ceremonial functions are, by implication, assigned to them there as they would be expected to fulfill in a papal cortège. The principal assignment is that of being in attendance upon the successors of the Apostles.

It follows from their assigned rôles and functions that all matters concerning precedence with regard to other Orders of Knighthood participating in ecclesiastical functions must be seen in this context. Papal Knights, when in attendance upon the successors of the Apostles, are part of the pontifical or episcopal curia or sacerdotal entourage. It would be alien to their assigned functions and rôle to involve themselves in such temporal matters as precedence between other Orders of Knighthood. This is clearly laid down in the high honour granted them by St. Pius X and, indeed, by being created a Papal Knight by the Supreme Pontiff.

Outside the framework of religious functions, Papal Knights take the place of precedence due to them according to the date of foundation of the Order.

The true rôle of a Papal Knight was clearly defined by His Eminence Cardinal Casaroli who reminded Papal Knights that they had not merely received a title of honour but taken on the duty of fighting evil, injustice and oppression.

CHAPTER TWO

BECOMING A PAPAL KNIGHT

An application for a gentleman to receive a Papal Knighthood can be made initially to the Ordinary of the Diocese in which the candidate proposed for the honour resides. Besides the Ordinary, who can propose a candidate himself, applications can be made by a Parish Priest or a Catholic organisation. The letter proposing a candidate for a knightly honour should be addressed to the Pope. This letter is first sent to the Apostolic Nuncio with the request for a *Nihil Obstat* and then forwarded to the Papal Secretariat of State.

If the application is approved, the Secretariat of State informs the Ordinary in due course and sends him the Papal Brief of appointment through diplomatic channels.

Papal Briefs for the Supreme Order of Christ, the Order of the Golden Spur, the Golden Collar of the Order of Pius IX and often the Knight Grand Cross of the Pontifical Equestrian Orders are signed personally by the Supreme Pontiff. Papal Briefs for Knights Commander and Knights of the Pontifical Equestrian Orders are signed by the Cardinal Secretary of State.

According to the Order of Knighthood and the rank to which a gentleman is appointed or promoted, the Secretariat of State, exercising its function as the successor to the Chancellery of the Pontifical Equestrian Orders, levies a tax on the Papal Brief. This tax, which is payable by the applicant, contributes to the administrative costs involved in the procedure. If the application for a Knighthood is made by a Parish Priest, he will be informed by the Local Bishop of the charges due. He pays the tax to the Diocese or Archdiocese, which in turn pays such taxes half-yearly to the Apostolic Nunciature which forwards it in due course to the Secretariat of State.

All Metropolitans and Diocesan Bishops regularly receive information from the Secretariat of State with regard to the amount of tax due on Papal Briefs bestowing a knightly honour. This information is also published in the *Acta Apostolicae Sedis.* The applicant is responsible for the payment of the tax on the Papal Brief and not the candidate.

The responsibility for providing the decoration, the miniature, lapel button and the uniform does not rest with the Holy See or the applicant, though the Local Bishop or the applicant usually acquires the decoration for the presentation. A Papal Knighthood which is conferred *motu proprio,* however, is not subject to tax, and the insignia are presented as a gift from the Supreme Pontiff through the Secretariat of State.

It is a matter for the applicant or the Ordinary to decide whether to bear the cost of the decoration as well as the taxes, or to advise the new or promoted Knight to acquire the decoration himself.

To ensure that the correct insignia are obtained, it is strongly recommended that the decoration is bought from a reputable dealer or manufacturer. In recent years a number of companies have entered the "order business", offering cut-price decorations. The crosses often bear little likeness to the correct decoration as described in the statutes of the Order. Decorations conferred *motu proprio* and given by the Holy See are acquired from Ditta Cravanzola, Via del Corso, 340–341, I–00186 Rome, Italy. Sig. Gardino of Messrs. Cravanzola will send an illustrated leaflet of the various decorations, miniatures, and lapel buttons of the Orders of St. Gregory the Great and Pope St. Sylvester and a price list on request. If in doubt when purchasing decorations for Pontifical Equestrian Orders from other firms in Italy or other countries, it would be prudent to insist on decorations, miniatures and lapel buttons which have been manufactured by Ditta Cravanzola.

A tax is also levied on the two Pontifical Awards of Merit, the Medal *Benemerenti* and the Cross *Pro Ecclesia et Pontifice*, but the Secretariat of State supplies the decorations with the Diploma. However, the Awards of Merit do not arrive with miniatures. These have been manufactured by Ditta Cravanzola, but can also be obtained from Spink & Son Ltd., King Street, St. James's, London S.W.1. As both awards hold Pontifical status, they may be worn at all public functions after permission has been obtained from the Head of State.

Details concerning uniforms for Papal Knights are in the statutes of the Order, a copy of which will be given to the candidate together with the Papal Brief. An English translation of these rules can be found in Chapter Three of this book.

Without advocating a monopoly, it is recommended that Knights who wish to acquire a uniform should do so from the Pontifical Tailors, Ditta Annibale Gammarelli, Via Santa Chiara 34, I–00186 Rome, Italy. The Secretaries of national Associations of Papal Knights can usually provide details on request. There is no need to go to Rome for a fitting; a diagram with the correct measurements sent to Messrs. Gammarelli is sufficient. There is a choice of two cloths: a heavy wool material and a light-weight wool cloth. The cost for the uniform is always borne by the Knight himself. The uniform, sword with frog, and cocked hat are not inexpensive, but as in the case of the decorations, quality and the correct style of the uniform are important factors to bear in mind. Besides the rules promulgated in 1905 concerning uniforms, additional hints and suggestions are given at the end of Chapter Three.

The wearing of the uniform is optional for Papal Knights, though they are encouraged to acquire one in order to participate fully in the activities of their Order and represent it at religious ceremonies and other functions.

There remain two more necessary administrative matters: the gazetting of the bestowal of the Papal Knighthood in the *Acta Apostolicae Sedis*, (the official bulletin of the Holy See,) and the application to the Sovereign or Head of State for permission to wear the insignia of the relevant papal honour.

The gazetting in the *Acta Apostolicae Sedis* of Knighthoods bestowed by the Supreme Pontiff takes place at the sole direction of the Secretariat of State after all administrative requirements have been fulfilled.

Application to the Sovereign or Head of State for permission to wear the insignia is made through the Protocol Department of the Government concerned. In Great Britain it is in the Foreign and Commonwealth Office. This can be done by the newly appointed Knight, writing to the Foreign Office, enclosing a photocopy of the Papal Brief and giving relevant information to the Protocol Department, which will forward the letter to the Sovereign's Private Secretary or, in a Republic, to the President's office. The applicant will in due course receive the decision; two kinds of permission can be granted: restricted and unrestricted. In countries where the Holy See is represented by an Apostolic Nuncio, permission might also be sought by writing to the Apostolic Nunciature and asking for the courtesy of Nuncio's help in applying to the Foreign Office for permission to wear the papal insignia.

Until such a permission is received, Papal Knights enjoy the rights and privileges conferred upon them by the Pope, including the wearing of the uniform and decorations for ecclesiastical purposes only.

In one respect the bestowal of papal honours differs from all other foreign decorations: because of the special status accorded to the Supreme Pontiff, the Pope is the only Sovereign who may confer honours without the preliminary procedure which would require the accredited ambassador to the Holy See or the Holy See's ambassador accredited to the recipient's country, to apply for permission for an honour to be bestowed prior to conferment.

The *Acta Apostolicae Sedis* in its present form dates from the decree by Pope St, Pius X of 29 June 1908. From 1865 until 1908 a periodical with the title *Acta Sanctae Sedis* published the main papal documents, but it lacked centralised control and omissions occurred. Omissions of names of new

Papal Knights in the *Acta Apostolicae Sedis* still occur on occasion; however, there usually is a simple administrative reason. For example, a Papal Knighthood will only be gazetted after the tax for the Papal Brief has been received by the Secretariat of State, and bearing in mind that this process can take up to fifteen months, there could be a delay of eighteen months before a notice appears.

It would be inappropriate to apply the same criteria to the bestowal of a Pontifical Knighthood as, for example, those for Knighthoods bestowed by the Sovereign in the United Kingdom . . . Apart from honours which are in the personal gift of the Sovereign, such as the Royal Victorian Order, or where special circumstances require an honour to be conferred by-passing the usual procedure, those to be honoured are gazetted in the annual New Year's List or in the Sovereign's official Birthday List. A person who is gazetted on 1 January as the recipient of a Knighthood, may as from midnight use the appellation "Sir" and the post-nominal letters of his Order and rank. He is a Knight as soon as he is gazetted, regardless of when the investiture takes place. The Royal Letters Patent bear the date of the gazetting.

A Papal Brief appointing a Knight, however, could have been dated in November of a particular year, arrive in the diplomatic pouch at the Apostolic Nunciature in May the next year, and then be forwarded to the Ordinary. The newly appointed Knight might learn of his appointment in June and be invested in September.

The date of appointment to the Order which will eventually be gazetted in the *Acta Apostolicae Sedis* is that on the Papal Brief. If a Knight is concerned that he has not been gazetted eighteen months after receiving the Papal Brief, he may ask the Apostolic Nunciature to make enquiries on his behalf. On the back of Papal Briefs appointing a Knight there is usually a number written in pencil. That is the reference number of the document, and it is useful to refer to it when making enquiries at the Apostolic Nunciature.

Permission by the Sovereign for a British subject to wear the papal insignia of the knighthood bestowed on him is received by a letter from the Principal Private Secretary of the Sovereign and is also announced in the *London Gazette*, the official bulletin which is published four times a week. The Knight may now wear his insignia publicly and in the presence of the Sovereign and Members of the Royal Family.

Insignia and decorations of Catholic Orders of Knighthood which have no *express* pontifical status, rank as 'Badges of Religion' and may only be worn at religious and private functions, as indeed may decorations which cannot receive permission to be worn because the grantor of the decoration is not represented by an ambassador in the country of the applicant. This ruling can cause embarrassment in cases where an honour is bestowed, for example, by a King, who has not abdicated but has been exiled, or a King's legitimate successor who is the Head of a Royal House. Exiled Monarchs and legitimate Heads of non-regnant Royal Houses are recognised as such by most countries and are accorded all the courtesies. Similarly acknowledged are the Dynastic Orders belonging to those Royal Houses, but they may only be worn at private functions, and no permission to wear them at State or royal functions is normally granted. As soon as a new political regime has established diplomatic relations, only the Orders and decorations of the new regime can be applied for to be worn at Court or at functions attended by members of the royal family, or, in a Republic, in the presence of the President.

It is known that legitimate decorations are on occasion worn at official functions although they have not received the Sovereign's permission to be worn; it was explained to me that in specific circumstances these decorations are 'tolerated' rather than expressly allowed.

For example, among the Dynastic Orders, those of King Constantine of the Hellenes must obviously create some embarrassment. Because they are not Catholic Orders of Knighthood I have chosen them to demonstrate clearly that these restrictions do not only apply to Catholic Orders but generally. The King had left Greece to go into voluntary exile in 1967, but his constitutional position remained unsettled until 1974, when a Republic was established. The change of government and constitution has no bearing on the legitimacy of the Dynastic Orders; most members of royal families in Europe and others whom the King has honoured wear the decorations. The question whether or not the Orders conferred by the King, who is now deprived of ambassadors and cannot apply through diplomatic channels for recipients to wear the legitimate insignia of his Dynastic Orders of Knighthood, has not as yet been satisfactorily resolved.

Another delicate problem exists in the case of the Polish Order of *Polonia Restituta*; throughout the second World War and for some time after, the Polish Government-in-exile was the only Polish Government recognised by the Western Governments, including the Holy See. Some of them had diplomatic representatives of the Government-in-exile accredited until the 1970s. The Polish Government-in-exile still has its headquarters in London, and the Polish President-in-exile is the Grand Master of the Catholic-founded Order of the White Eagle and of the Order of *Polonia Restituta*, the legitimate successor to the Catholic-founded Order of St. Stanislaus. However, the Polish Government in Warsaw also confers the Order of *Polonia Restituta*, but based on a new, secular constitution. As I explain elsewhere, although the British Foreign Office only accepts applications to wear this decoration through diplomatic channels of the Polish People's Republic, many other countries make no distinction between the two grantors.

As far as Catholic Religious Orders of Knighthood are concerned, the Equestrian Order of the Holy Sepulchre of Jerusalem, an Order under the protection of the Holy See, has no *express* Pontifical status. I merely note that the insignia and awards of merit of this Order may be worn unrestricted in almost all European countries. In Great Britain, permission to wear them is restricted to religious and private functions.

Somewhat paradoxical is the position of the Sovereign Military Order of Malta which has over fifty ambassadors accredited to it in Rome and has its own ambassadors accredited to them on a reciprocal basis; among them are Italy, Spain and Portugal who are members of the EEC. The Order also has three delegates accredited to other Common Market countries, Belgium, France and the Federal Republic of Germany. The Order's insignia and the Order *Pro Merito Melitensi* are fully recognised and even worn by serving members of the armed forces of these EEC countries. The Order is a member of several United Nations committees and has its permanent observer at the Council of Europe. In the United Kingdom, neither insignia nor the Order of Merit are given permission to be worn at State functions. This is particularly amazing if one looks at the photograph on page 80 in *Orders of Knighthood, Awards and the Holy See* which shows the British Sovereign, King Edward VII, wearing the Grand Cross of Honour and Devotion of the Sovereign Military Order of Malta during his visit to Malta in 1907.

The Sacred and Military Constantinian Order of St. George (Two Sicilies) is fully recognised by the Holy See as a Catholic Order of Knighthood under the Grand Mastership of the Duke of Castro and had a Cardinal appointed to it as 'Personal Representative of the Supreme Pontiff'. It is also fully recognised as an Order of Knighthood by the Italian Republic, the President of which accepted in 1986 the Grand Cross and Collar of the Order. Early in 1987, the Constantinian Order was discussed in the learned journal of the Orders and Medals Research Society (Great Britain), the Patron of which is H.R.H. The Prince of Wales. The writer mentioned the Order's strong link with the Holy See and at the same time its excellent relations with the Italian Republic, and two possible developments were predicted: The S.M. Constantinian Order of St. George might in the not too distant future be represented at ambassadorial level by the Apostolic Nuncio to the European Economic Community, or enter into relations with the Republic which would represent the Order abroad through the Italian ambassadors. In either case, the Constantinian Order could be the first Dynastic Order under the

Grand Mastership of a non regnant Head of a Royal House to be granted full recognition in all the countries of the European Economic Community, including Great Britain. As Desmond Seward, the historian and author, points out in his *Italy's Knights of St. George*, it is because of religious reasons that only few British subjects have been eligible for membership of the Order. Nevertheless, Englishmen and Scots have belonged to it from an early date; a Captain William D'Arley, who was created a Knight of Grace of the Constantinian Order of St. George in 1801, obtained a Royal Licence from King George III to style himself 'Sir William'. In Great Britain the Order has a National Association under the presidency of the Premier Baron of England, The Lord Mowbray, Segrave and Stourton, CBE.

Unlike the Knights of the other Catholic Orders of Chivalry, the Knights of the Pontifical Equestrian Orders are represented in Great Britain at ambassadorial level by the Apostolic Pro-Nuncio to the Court of St. James. Besides being granted permission to wear their uniform and decorations unrestricted, as soon as permission has been received from the British Sovereign, the Knights, Knights Commander and Knights Grand Cross are entitled to use post-nominal letters which are used after any post-nominal letters of British Orders.

Because only the Earl Marshal of England has received the Pian Order, no post-nominal letters have been devised for the Order of Pius IX, but the post-nominal letters which are in common use are, for the Order of St. Gregory the Great: K.S.G. (Knight), K.C.S.G. (Knight Commander) and G.C.S.G. (Knight Grand Cross); for the Order of Pope St. Sylvester: K.S.S. (Knight), K.C.S.S. (Knight Commander) and G.C.S.S. (Knight Grand Cross).

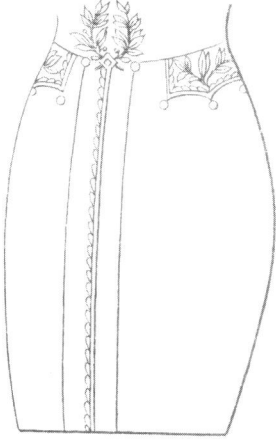

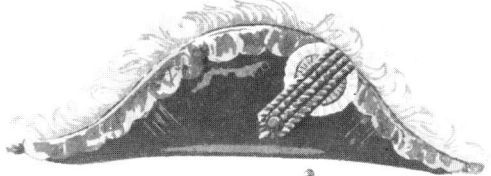

CHAPTER THREE

I

THE PONTIFICAL EQUESTRIAN ORDER
OF PIUS IX — THE PIAN KNIGHTS

FROM THE CHANCERY OF THE PONTIFICAL
EQUESTRIAN ORDERS

February 1905

HIS HOLINESS POPE PIUS X, having given consideration to all the mandates of the Holy See promulgated to encourage virtue and to reward good conduct, wishing such rewards to be fitting and proper and, indeed, honour the Holy See itself, has on this occasion turned His attention to the Orders of Knighthood.

Hence, having discussed the matter with the undersigned Cardinal Secretary of Briefs, the Grand Chancellor of the Pontifical Orders of Knighthood, He has promulgated, besides all the regulations given this day to the other Pontifical Orders of Knighthood, all those rules concerning the uniform and decorations of the Knights of the Order of Pius IX (The Pian Knights), which have until now appeared ambiguous and lacking clear definition, and He has ordered that these matters be precisely defined according to the following regulations: —

PIAN KNIGHTS OF THE FIRST CLASS or KNIGHTS GRAND CROSS OF THE ORDER OF PIUS IX shall enjoy the privilege of hereditary nobility, which may be inherited by their sons.

Their uniform should be of dark blue cloth with coat-tails.

The collar, the cuffs and the pockets should be of red cloth.

The embroidery, all in gold thread, should be a row of laurel leaves on the collar, on the cuffs and on the pockets. There should be a double row of laurel leaves on the chest and also a narrow gilt border decorated with laurel leaves, which runs along the top and front of the collar, down the centre, along the edge of the pocket flaps, the top and side of the cuffs and along the edge of the entire tailcoat.

There should be nine buttons on the chest and three smaller buttons on each sleeve. The tail of the coat which borders on the pocket flaps should be adorned with two larger buttons, and in the centre, above the buttons should be two embroidered sprays of laurel leaves arranged in an oval circlet. At the three protruding points of the pocket flaps there should be three small buttons.

On both shoulders should be a golden braid, fastened near the collar with a button.

The trousers should be long and of dark blue cloth. A gold stripe decorated with laurel leaves, four centimetres in width, should run down the outer sides of the trousers.

The cocked hat should be of black plush velvet, adorned with a broad gold band along the top rim, with a small golden tassel at either end, and above there should be a white plume, to which the Pontifical Cockade is attached on the right side, held by four intertwined strands of gold cord and fastened at the lower end with a gilded button.

The buttons, all gilded, should be embossed with the Badge of the Order. The court sword should be worn in a sword frog, made of golden braid decorated with laurel leaves. The sword should bear on the hilt the badge of the Order. The handle should be of mother of pearl with gilded mounts and with a gilt sword-knot hanging from it. The scabbard should be of black leather with gilt boss and ferrule.

The Badge of the Order is an eight-pointed blue star superimposed on an eight-pointed star-like cluster of seven rays, each in gold, and a white enamel medallion with a broad gold border which is silver-rimmed. In the inner white circle is the name of the Founder, PIUS IX, and in the gold border is the inscription VIRTUTI ET MERITO.

The Star should be the eight-pointed blue star superimposed on an eight-pointed silver star-like cluster of rays, eight centimetres in diameter, and it is worn on the left side of the breast.

A Knight Grand Cross wears the Badge, six and a half centimetres in diameter, suspended from a sash, ten centimetres wide, which is of a dark blue moiré with two red stripes along both borders.

The Badge, Star and buttons, according to their shape and sizes, and sash, bands and stripes, according to colour and width should not vary from the patterns and designs given.

PIAN KNIGHTS OF THE SECOND CLASS OR KNIGHTS COMMANDER OF THE ORDER OF PIUS IX shall enjoy the honour of personal nobility which is not hereditary.

Their uniform should be of dark blue cloth with coat-tails.

The collar, the cuffs and the pockets should be of red cloth.

The embroidery, all in gold thread, should be a row of laurel leaves on the collar, on the cuffs and on the pockets, and a narrow gilt border,

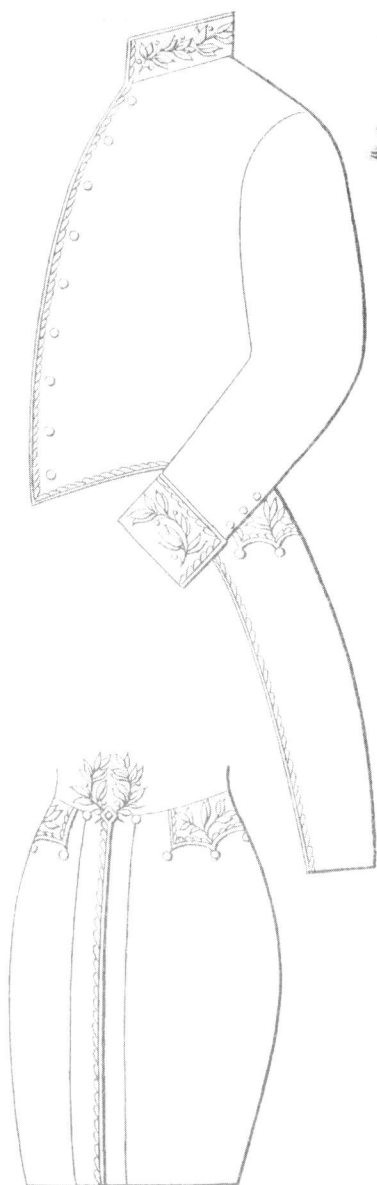

deocrated with laurel leaves, which runs along the top and front of the collar, down the front, along the edge of the pocket flaps, on the top and side of the cuffs and along the edge of the entire tailcoat.

There should be nine buttons on the chest and three smaller buttons on each sleeve. The tail of the coat which borders on the pocket flaps should be adorned with two larger buttons, and in the centre, above the buttons should be two embroidered sprays of laurel leaves arranged in an oval circlet. At the three protruding points of the pocket flaps should be three small buttons.

The trousers should be long and of dark blue cloth. A gold stripe decorated with'laurel leaves, four centimetres in width, should run down the outer sides of the trousers.

The cocked hat should be of black plush velvet, adorned with two black silk bands running diagonally at either end and on both sides from the upper rim of the hat to the lower part, and a third black silk band running along the top rim, with gilt tassels on both corners. The hat is surmounted with a black plume, to which the Pontifical Cockade is attached on the right side, held by four strands of intertwined gold cord and fastened at the lower end with a gilded button.

The buttons, all gilded, should be embossed with the Badge of the Order. The court sword should be worn in a sword frog, made of gold braid with laurel leaves. The sword should bear on the hilt the Badge of the Order. The handle should be of mother of pearl with gilded mounts and with a gilt sword-knot hanging from it; the scabbard should be of black leather with gilt boss and ferrule.

The Badge of the Order is an eight-pointed blue star superimposed on an eight-pointed star-like cluster of seven gold rays each, and a white enamel medallion with a broad gold border which is silver-rimmed. In the inner white circle is the name of the Founder, PIUS IX, and in the gold border is the inscription VIRTUTI ET MERITO.

A Knight Commander wears his Badge, six centimetres in diameter, on a neck riband, five centimetres wide, of dark blue moiré with two red stripes on each border.

A Knight Commander *con placca* wears in addition an eight-pointed blue Star, superimposed on a star-like cluster of seven rays in silver, seven centimetres in diameter, on the left side of his breast.

The Badge of the Order and buttons, according to their shape and sizes, and the riband, bands and stripes, according to colour and width, should not vary from the patterns and designs given.

For PIAN KNIGHTS OF THE THIRD CLASS or KNIGHTS OF THE

ORDER OF PIUS IX the uniform should be of dark blue cloth with coat-tails.

The collar, the cuffs and the pockets should be of red cloth.

The decoration should be a narrow gilt border, decorated with laurel leaves, at the top and front of the collar, at the top and side of the cuffs, running along the edge of the pockets and along the edge of the entire tailcoat.

There should be nine buttons on the chest and three smaller ones on each sleeve. The tail of the coat which borders on the pocket flaps should be adorned with two larger buttons, and in the centre, above the buttons should be two embroidered sprays of laurel leaves in gold thread arranged in a narrow oval circlet. At the three protruding points of the pockets should be three small buttons.

The trousers should be long and of dark blue cloth. A gold stripe, three centimetres wide, decorated with laurel leaves, should run down the outer sides of the trousers.

The cocked hat should be of black plush velvet, adorned with two black silk bands running diagonally on either end and on both sides from the upper rim of the hat to the lower part, and a third black silk band running along the upper rim. The hat should be surmounted by a black plume to which the Pontifical Cockade is attached on the right side, held by four strands of intertwined gold cord and fastened at the lower end with a gilded button.

The buttons, all gilded, should be embossed with the Badge of the Order. The court sword should be worn in a sword frog of golden braid, decorated with laurel leaves. The sword should bear on the hilt the Badge of the Order. The handle should be of mother of pearl with gilded mounts and with a gilt sword-knot hanging from it. The scabbard should be of black leather with gilt boss and ferrule.

The Badge of the Order is an eight-pointed blue star superimposed on an eight-pointed cluster of seven gold rays each, and a white enamel medallion with a broad gold border which is silver-rimmed. In the white circle is the name of the Founder, PIUS IX, and in the golden border is the inscription VIRTUTI ET MERITO.

A Knight of the Order of Pius IX wears the Badge five centimetres in diameter, on a dark blue ribbon with two red stripes on both sides of the border, three and a half centimetres wide, on his left breast.

The Badge and buttons, according to their shape and sizes, and the ribbon, bands and stripes, according to colour and width, should not vary from the patterns and designs given.

LUIGI CARD. MACCHI
Grand Chancellor of the Pontifical Equestrian Orders

45

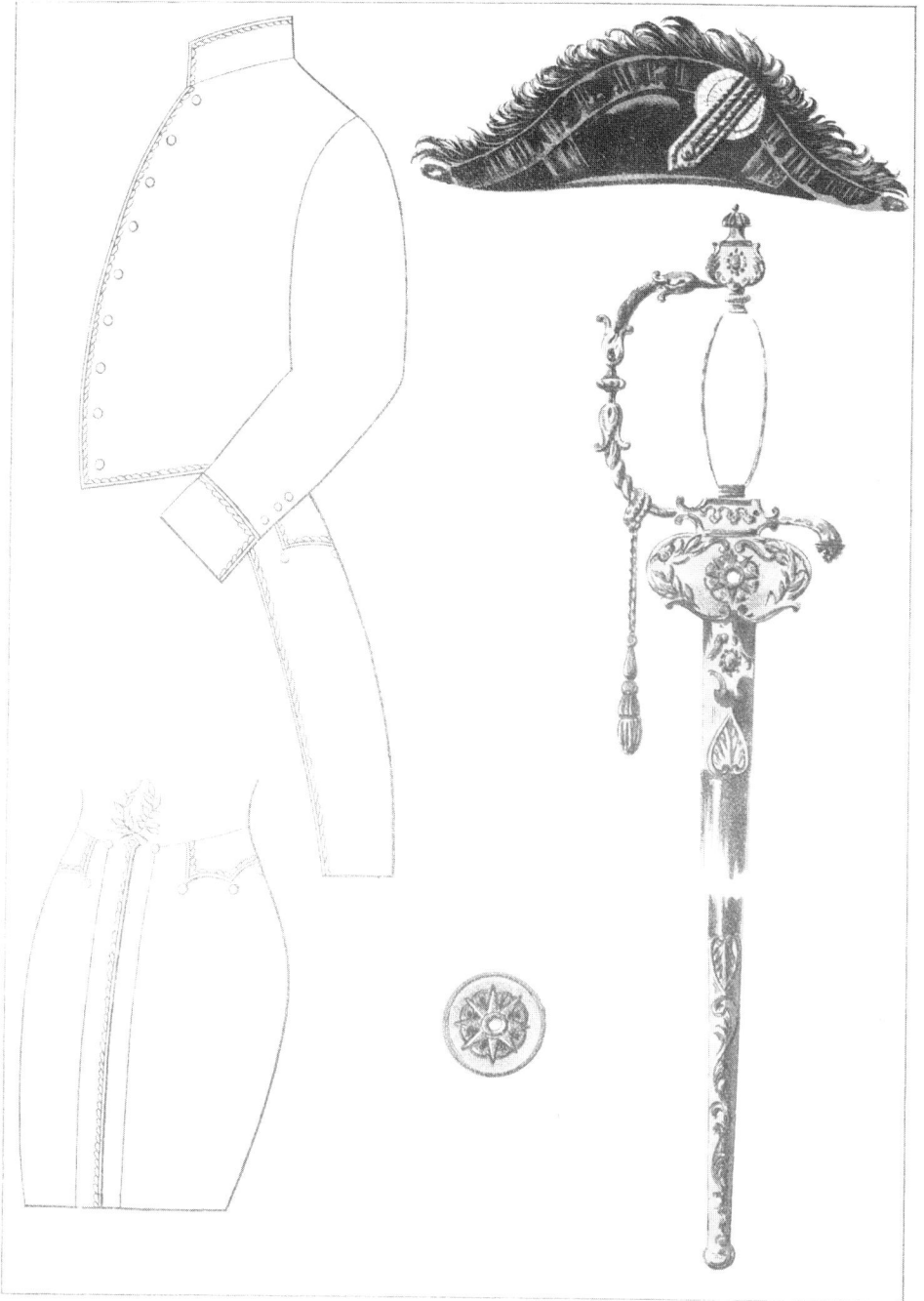

PAPAL BRIEF OF PIUS XII P.P. CONCERNING THE ABOLITION OF NOBILITY CONFERRED WITH THE ORDER OF PIUS IX.

FOR PERPETUAL REMEMBRANCE. Our Predecessor, Pope Pius IX by His Apostolic Letters in the form of Papal Briefs, dates 17 June 1847 and 17 June 1849, and by His Decree given at the Quirinal on 11 November 1856, created and instituted the Equestrian Order known as Pian Knights, which was to have three Classes of Knights. By these same Apostolic Letters it was decreed that those admitted to the First Class of the Pian Order should also receive the privilege of hereditary nobility which could be inherited by their sons, whereas those admitted to the Second Class should receive the privilege of nobility *ad personam* only.

In order that the Pian Order, to use the words of Our memorable Predecessor, should have as its aim "not to foment vanity and ambition, but rather solely to reward virtue and outstanding merit", We have decided that the same criteria should apply as in all the other Pontifical Orders of Knighthood, none of which enjoy the privilege of nobility. Papal Knights who have excelled either in their gifts of mind and heart, who have shown conspicuous loyalty to the Holy See, or given meritorious service to the Church, are acknowledged and rewarded by their title of rank and their insignia proper to the Order of Knighthood.

After giving careful consideration to these matters, We have decided to decree in the Lord that the status of nobility which was decreed in the aforementioned Apostolic Letters be abolished, and that as from today each and everyone admitted to any of the three Classes of the Pian Knights may legitimately use only the title of their rank and the insignia of their Class, and the status of nobility is hereby excluded.

We therefore decide, notwithstanding anything to the contrary, that this Papal Brief shall for always be inviolable and efficacious and henceforth take its full and total effect. Thus one must judge and define from now on null and void any attempt that may be made by any authority whatever, whether knowingly or in ignorance, all that is contrary to what is stated above.

Given at St. Peter's in Rome, under the Seal of the Fisherman this eleventh Day of November 1939, in the first year of Our Pontificate.

L. CARD. MAGLIONE
Secretary of State

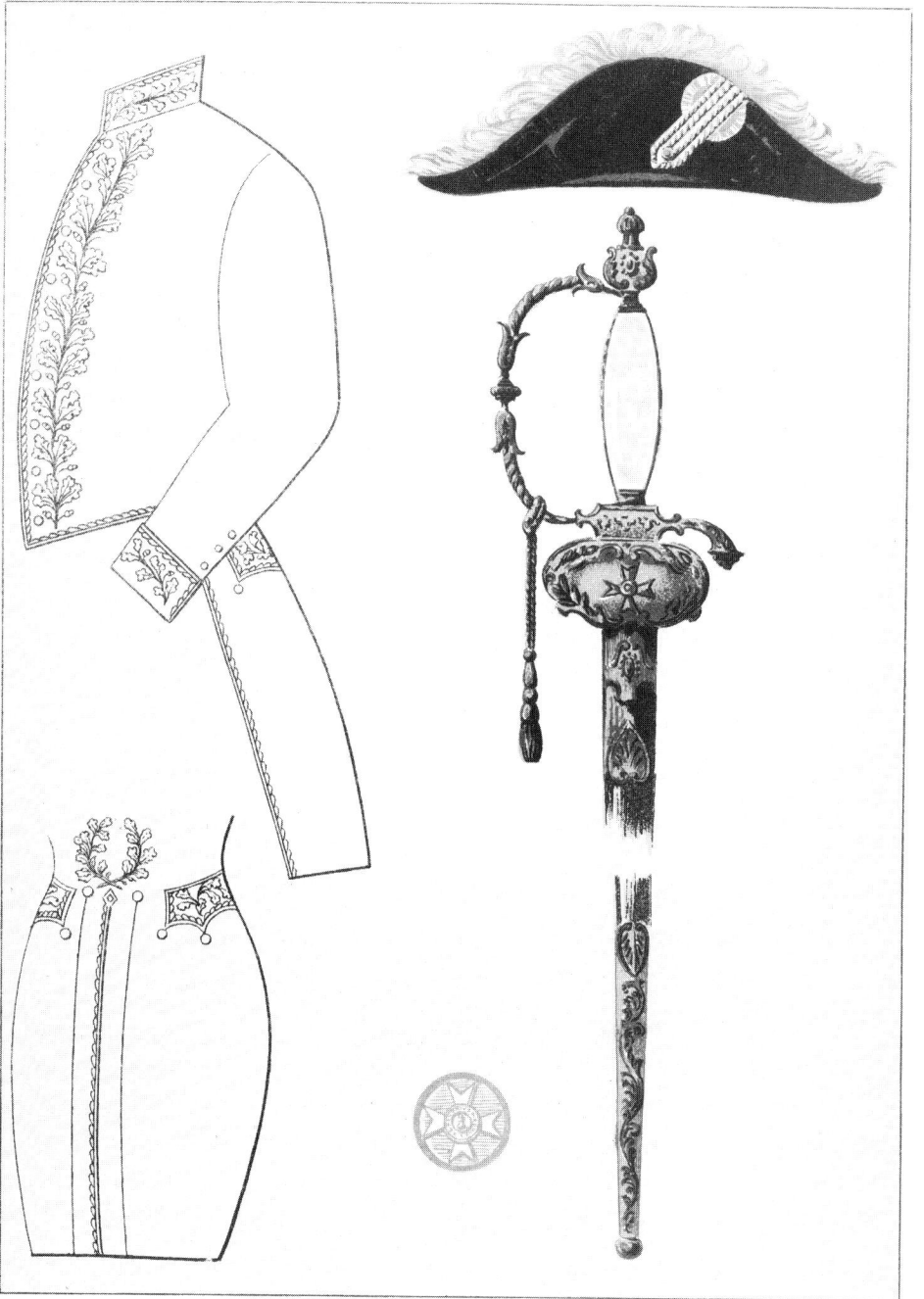

THE PONTIFICAL EQUESTRIAN ORDER OF ST. GREGORY THE GREAT

FROM THE CHANCERY OF THE PONTIFICAL EQUESTRIAN ORDERS

7 February 1905

HIS HOLINESS POPE PIUS X, having given consideration to all the mandates of the Holy See promulgated to encourage virtue and to reward good conduct, wishing such rewards to be fitting and proper and, indeed, honour the Holy See itself, has on this occasion turned His attention to the Orders of Knighthood.

Hence, having discussed the matter with the undersigned Cardinal Secretary of Briefs, the Grand Chancellor of the Pontifical Orders of Knighthood, He has promulgated, besides all the regulations given this day to the other Pontifical Orders of Knighthood, all those rules concerning the uniform and decorations and their use for THE ORDER OF ST. GREGORY THE GREAT, which have until now appeared ambiguous and lacking clear definition, and He has ordered that these matters be precisely defined according to the following regulations, retaining however, unchanged the provision of having two Classes: one for Civilians, the other for the Military.

KNIGHTS GRAND CROSS OF THE CIVILIAN CLASS OF THE ORDER OF ST. GREGORY THE GREAT

Their uniform should be of a dark green cloth with coat-tails.

The embroidery, all in silver thread, should be a row of oak-leaves on the collar, on the cuffs and on the pockets. There should be a double row of oakleaves on the chest and also a silver border with oakleaves which runs along the top edge and front of the collar, along the front in the centre of the uniform and the edge of the pockets flaps, the top and sides of the cuffs and along the edge of the entire tailcoat.

There should be nine buttons on the chest and three smaller buttons on each sleeve. The tail of the coat which borders on the pocket flaps should be adorned with two larger buttons, and in the centre, above the buttons should be two embroidered branches with oakleaves arranged in a circlet. At the three protruding points of the pocket-flaps there should be three small buttons.

On both shoulders should be a silver braid, fastened near the collar with a button.

The trousers should be long and of dark green cloth. A silver stripe decorated with oakleaves, four centimetres in width, should run down the outer sides of the trousers.

The cocked hat should be of black plush velvet, adorned with a silver band along the top rim, and with a small silver tassel at either end, and above there should be a white plume, to which the Pontifical Cockade is attached on the right side, held by four intertwined strands of silver cord and fastened at the lower end with a silver button.

The buttons, all in silver, should be embossed with the Cross of the Order. The court sword should be worn in a sword frog, made of silver braid decorated with oakleaves. The sword should bear on the hilt the Cross of the Order (without the laurel wreath). The handle should be of mother of pearl with gilded mounts and with a gilt sword-knot hanging from it. The scabbard should be of black leather with gilt boss and ferrule.

The Cross of the Order (Civil Class) is an eight-pointed, gold-rimmed and ball-pointed Maltese cross of deep red enamel, with a blue medallion bearing the image of St. Gregory the Great in gold relief, and in a gold circle the inscription S. GREGORIUS MAGNUS. On the reverse side are the words PRO DEO ET PRINCIPE. The Cross is surmounted by a wreath of gold-rimmed, green enamelled oakleaves, tied at the bottom with a golden bow.

A Knight Grand Cross wears the Cross, six and a half centimetres in diameter, surmounted by the laurel wreath, three and a half centimetres wide and three centimetres deep, suspended from a sash, ten centimetres wide, which is of scarlet moiré with a yellow border either side.

The Star of a Knight Grand Cross is the Cross of the above size (but without the laurel wreath) superimposed on an eight pointed silver star, eight and a half centimetres in diameter, which is worn on the left side.

The Cross, Star and buttons, according to their shape and sizes, and the sash, bands and stripes, according to colour and width, should not vary from the patterns and designs given.

KNIGHTS COMMANDER OF THE CIVILIAN CLASS OF THE ORDER OF ST. GREGORY THE GREAT

Their uniform should be of a dark green cloth with coat-tails.

The embroidery, all in silver thread, should be a row of oakleaves on the collar, on the cuffs and on the pockets, and a silver border with oakleaves which runs along the top edge and front of the collar, down the centre of the uniform and along the edge of the entire tailcoat, along the edge of the pocket flaps and the top and side of the cuffs.

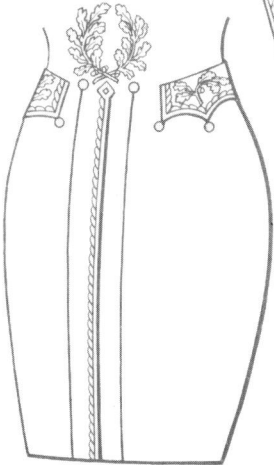

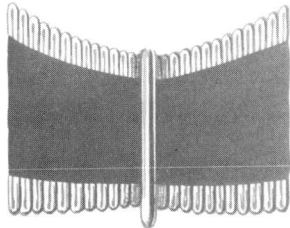

There should be nine buttons on the chest and three smaller buttons on each sleeve. The tail of the coat which borders on the pocket flaps should be adorned with two larger buttons, and in the centre, above the buttons should be two embroidered branches with oakleaves arranged in a circlet. At the three protruding points of the pocket-flaps there should be three small buttons.

The trousers should be long and of dark green cloth. A silver stripe decorated with oakleaves, four centimetres in width, should run down the outer sides of the trousers.

The cocked hat should be of black plush velvet, adorned with two black silk bands running diagonally at either end and on both sides from the upper rim of the hat to the lower part, and a third black silk band running along the top rim, with a small silver tassel at either end. The hat should be surmounted with a black plume, to which the Pontifical Cockade is attached on the right side, held by four intertwined strands of silver cord and fastened at the lower end with a silver button.

The buttons, all in silver, should be embossed with the Cross of the Order. The court sword should be worn in a sword frog, made of silver braid decorated with oakleaves. The sword should bear on the hilt the Cross of the Order (without the laurel wreath). The handle should be of mother of pearl with gilded mounts and with a gilt sword-knot hanging from it. The scabbard should be of black leather with gilt boss and ferrule.

The Cross of the Order (Civil Class) is an eight-pointed, gold-rimmed and ball-pointed Maltese cross of deep red enamel, with a blue medallion bearing the image of St. Gregory the Great in gold relief, and in a gold circle the inscription S. GREGORIUS MAGNUS. On the reverse side are the words PRO DEO ET PRINCIPE. The Cross is surmounted by a wreath of gold-rimmed, green enamelled oakleaves, tied at the bottom with a golden bow.

A Knight Commander wears his Cross, six and a half centimetres in diameter, on a neck riband, five centimetres wide, of scarlet moiré with yellow borders.

A Knight Commander *con placca* wears in addition a smaller eight-pointed silver star, seven centimetres in diameter, on which is superimposed the Cross of the Order, five centimetres in diameter, on the left side of his breast.

The Cross of the Order and buttons, according to their shape and sizes, and the riband, bands and stripes, according to colour and width, should not vary from the patterns and designs given.

KNIGHTS OF THE CIVILIAN CLASS
OF THE ORDER OF ST. GREGORY THE GREAT

Their uniform should be of a dark green cloth with coat-tails.

The silver decoration should be a border with oakleaves along the top edge and front of the collar, on the cuffs and on the edge of the pocket flaps, and which runs along the front of the uniform and along the edge of the entire tail coat.

There should be nine buttons on the chest and three smaller buttons on each sleeve. The tail of the coat which borders on the pocket flaps should be adorned with two larger buttons, and in the centre, above the buttons should be two branches with oakleaves, embroidered in silver thread and arranged in a circlet. At the three protruding points of the pocket flaps there should be three small buttons.

The trousers should be long and of dark green cloth. A silver stripe decorated with oakleaves, three centimetres in width, should run down the outer sides of the trousers.

The cocked hat should be of black plush velvet, adorned with two black silk bands running diagonally at either end and on both sides from the upper rim of the hat to the lower part, and a third black silk band running along the upper rim with a small silver tassel at either end. The hat should be surmounted by a black plume to which the Pontifical Cockade is attached on the right side, held by four strands of intertwined silver cord and fastened at the lower end with a silver button.

The buttons, all in silver, should be embossed with the Cross of the Order. The court sword should be worn in a sword frog, made of silver braid decorated with oakleaves. The sword should bear on the hilt the Cross of the Order (without the laurel wreath). The handle should be of mother of pearl with gilded mounts and with a gilt sword-knot hanging from it. The scabbard should be of black leather with gilt boss and ferrule.

The Cross of the Order (Civil Class) is an eight-pointed, gold-rimmed and ball-pointed Maltese cross of deep red enamel, with a blue medallion bearing the image of St. Gregory the Great in gold relief, and in a gold circle the inscription S. GREGORIUS MAGNUS. On the reverse side are the words PRO DEO ET PRINCIPE. The Cross is surmounted by a wreath of gold-rimmed, green enamelled oakleaves, tied at the bottom with a golden bow.

A Knight of the Order wears the Cross, five centimetres in diameter, on a scarlet ribbon, three and a half centimetres wide, with yellow borders, on the left side of the chest.

The Cross and buttons, according to their shape and sizes, and the ribbon, bands and stripes, according to colour and width, should not vary from the

53

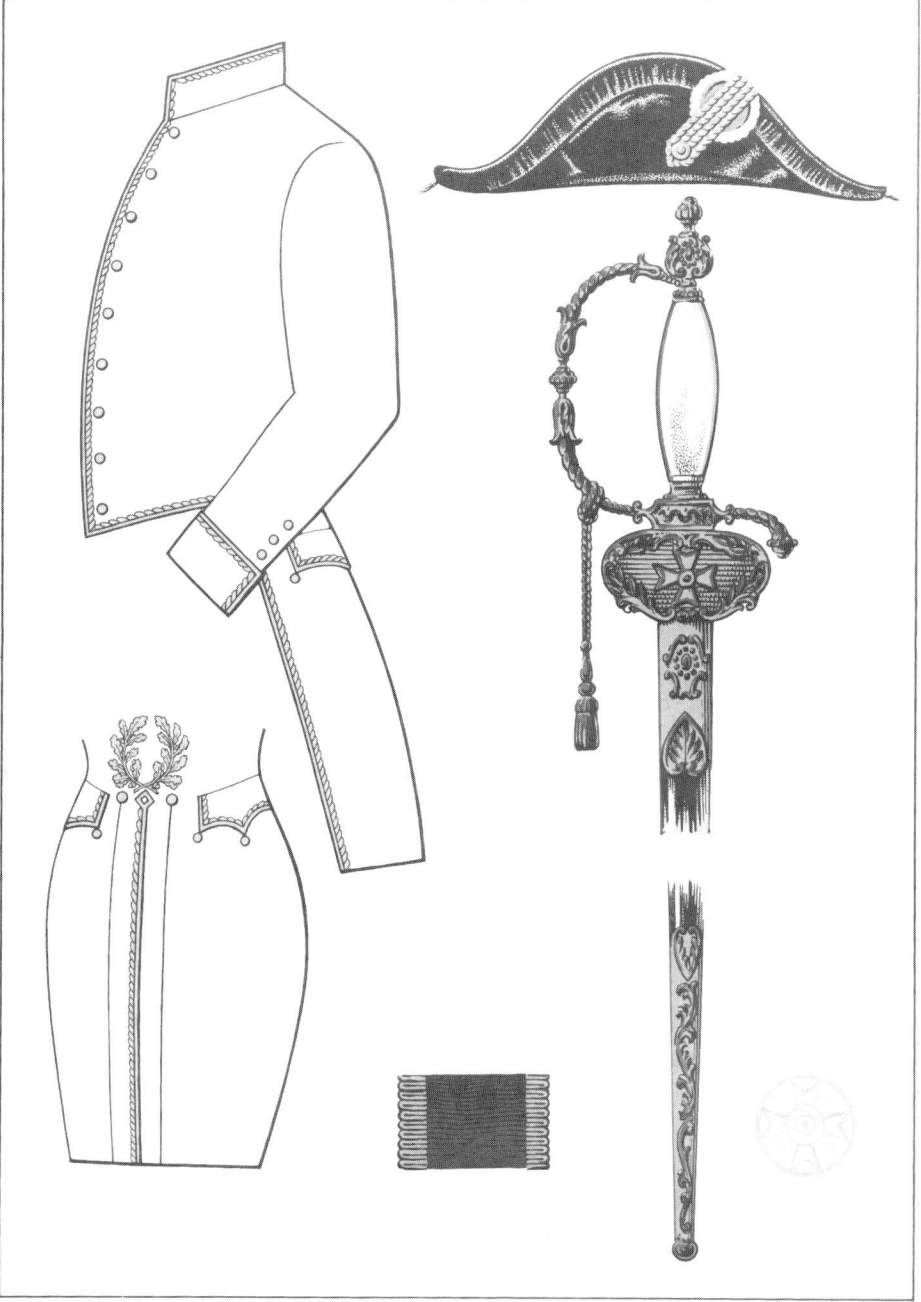

patterns and designs given.

KNIGHTS OF THE MILITARY CLASS are professional soldiers, either those who serve in the troops or guards of the Pope, or in the armed forces of any nation, but who for their outstanding service for God and the Supreme Pontiff, deserve to be specially honoured.

No special uniform is prescribed for Knights of the Military Class as they wear the uniforms of their own nations and regiments.

The Cross of the Order (Military Class) is an eight-pointed, gold-rimmed and ball-pointed Maltese cross in deep red enamel, with a blue medallion bearing the image of St. Gregory the Great in gold relief, and in a gold circle the inscription S. GREGORIUS MAGNUS. On the reverse side are the words PRO DEO ET PRINCIPE.

The Cross is surmounted by a gilded military trophy of the same depth and two thirds of the width of the Cross itself. It is for this reason that the Crosses in the respective ranks are smaller than in the equivalant ranks of the Civilian Class.

KNIGHTS GRAND CROSS OF THE MILITARY CLASS

Knights Grand Cross wear the Star of the Order, which is equivalent to that of the Civilian Class, on the left side of their breast. They have also the right to wear a Grand Cross, five centimetres in diameter, as a neck badge, suspended from a silk scarlet riband, five centimetres wide, with yellow borders.

KNIGHTS COMMANDER OF THE MILITARY CLASS

Knights Commander are entitled to wear the Cross, five centimetres in diameter, as a neck badge, suspended from a scarlet silk riband, five centimetres wide, with yellow borders.

Knights Commander *con placca* wear the identical star to that worn in the Civil Class on their left breast.

KNIGHTS OF THE MILITARY CLASS

Knights wear their Cross, three and a half centimetres in diameter, on the left side of their breast, suspended from a silk scarlet ribbon, three and a half centimetres wide, with yellow borders.

The Crosses, according to size and shape, and the riband and ribbon as to colour and width should not differ from the designs laid down.

LUIGI CARD. MACCHI
Grand Chancellor of the Pontifical Equestrian Orders

THE PONTIFICAL EQUESTRIAN ORDER OF POPE ST. SYLVESTER

FROM THE CHANCERY OF THE PONTIFICAL EQUESTRIAN ORDERS

7 February 1905

HIS HOLINESS POPE PIUS X, having given consideration to all the mandates of the Holy See promulgated to encourage virtue and to reward good conduct, wishing such rewards to be fitting and proper and, indeed, honour the Holy See itself, has on this occasion turned His attention to the Orders of Knighthood.

Hence, having discussed the matter with the undersigned Cardinal Secretary of Briefs, the Grand Chancellor of the Pontifical Orders of Knighthood, He has ordered, to the greater honour and memory of Pope St. Sylvester I, that the Pontifical Order of the Golden Militia and St. Sylvester, according to the Apostolic Brief of His Predecessor the late Pope Gregory XVI, dated 31 October 1841, shall change its name henceforth, and no longer join it to another Order of Knighthood, but that the Order shall be known only by the name of His Holy Predecessor, Pope St. Sylvester, the first patron of Christian Chivalry; and He decrees further that like the other Pontifical Equestrian Orders, it shall not only comprise Knights and Knights Commander but also Knights Grand Cross. He has ordered in an Apostolic Letter which bears today's date, that matters pertaining to the honours, privileges, uniform and head-dress be precisely defined according to the following regulations: —

KNIGHTS GRAND CROSS OF THE ORDER OF POPE ST. SYLVESTER

Their uniform should be of black cloth with coat-tails.

The collar and cuffs should be of black velvet.

The embroidery, all in gold thread, should be a row of laurel leaves on the collar, on the cuffs and on the pockets. There should be a double row of laurel leaves on the chest, and also a narrow gilt border, decorated with laurel leaves, along the top edge and front of the collar, surround the pocket flaps and run along the edge and side of the cuffs.

There should be nine buttons on the chest and three smaller buttons on each sleeve. The tail of the coat which borders on the pocket flaps should be adorned with two larger buttons, and in the centre, above the buttons, should be two embroidered sprays of laurel leaves arranged in an oval circlet.

On both shoulders should be a twisted gilt cord, fastened near the collar with a button.

The trousers should be long and of black cloth. A gold stripe, four centimetres wide, decorated with laurel leaves, should run down the outer sides of the trousers.

The cocked hat should be of black heavy silk, adorned with two black bands running diagonally at either end and on both sides from the upper rim of the hat to the lower part, and a small gilt tassel should be at either end of the hat which is to be surmounted by a white plume to which the Pontifical Cockade is attached on the right side, held by four strands of intertwined gilded cord and fastened at the lower end with a gilded button.

The buttons, all gilded, should be embossed with the Cross of the Order. The court sword should be worn in a sword frog made of gold braid decorated with laurel leaves. The sword should bear on the hilt the Cross of the Order. The handle should be of mother of pearl with gilded mounts and with a gilt sword-knot hanging from it. The scabbard should be of black leather with gilt boss an ferrule.

The Cross of the Order is a gold-rimmed, eight-pointed, white enamel Maltese cross with four shorter clusters of eight gilded rays protruding between the arms of the Cross. In the centre of the Cross is a blue medallion with a silver-rimmed yellow border, bearing in gilt relief the image of Pope St. Sylvester wearing a tiara, and in the yellow border the words: SANC SILVESTER P.M.

The Knight Grand Cross wears the Cross, five centimetres in diameter, from a sash ten centimetres wide, which is of black moiré with three red stripes, one in the centre and one along each border.

The Star of a Knight Grand Cross is the Cross of the above size, superimposed on an eight-pointed silver star, eight centimetres in diameter, which is worn on the left side of the breast.

The Cross, Star and buttons, according to their shape and sizes, and the sash, bands and stripes, according to colour and width should not vary from the patterns and designs given.

KNIGHTS COMMANDER OF THE
ORDER OF POPE ST. SYLVESTER

Their uniform should be of black cloth with coat-tails.

The collar and cuffs should be of black velvet.

The embroidery, all in gold thread, should be a row of laurel leaves on the collar, on the cuffs and on the pockets, and a narrow gilt border, should run along the top edge and front of the collar, the top and on the side of the cuffs and surround the pocket flaps.

There should be nine buttons on the chest and three smaller buttons on each sleeve. The tail of the coat which borders on the pocket flaps should be adorned with two larger buttons, and in the centre, above the buttons, should be two embroidered sprays of laurel leaves arranged in an oval circlet.

The trousers should be long and of black cloth. A gold stripe, four centimetres wide, decorated with laurel leaves should run down the sides of the trousers.

The cocked hat should be of black thick silk, adorned with two black bands running diagonally at either end and on both sides from the upper rim of the hat to the lower part, with a small gold tassel at either end. The hat should be surmounted by a black plume to which the Pontifical Cockade is attached on the right side, held by four intertwined strands of gilded cord and fastened at the lower end with a gilded button.

The buttons, all gilded, should be embossed with the Cross of the Order. The court sword should be worn in a sword frog made of gilded braid decorated with laurel leaves. The sword should bear on the hilt the Cross of the Order. The handle should be of mother of pearl with gilded mounts and with a gilt sword-knot hanging from it. The scabbard should be of black leather with gilt boss an ferrule.

The Cross of the Order is a silver-rimmed, eight-pointed, white enamel Maltese cross with four clusters of eight shorter gilded rays protruding between the arms of the Cross. In the centre of the Cross is a blue medallion with a silver-rimmed yellow border, bearing in gilt relief the image of Pope St. Sylvester wearing a tiara, and in the yellow border the words: SANC SILVESTER P.M.

A Knight Commander wears his Cross, five centimetres in diameter, on a neck riband, five centimetres wide, of black moiré with three red stripes, one in the centre and one on each border.

A Knight Commander *con placca* wears in addition a smaller eight-pointed silver star, seven centimetres in diameter, on which a Cross, four

and a half centimetres in diameter is superimposed, and it is worn on the left side of the breast.

The Cross, Star and buttons, according to their shape and sizes, and the riband, bands and stripes, according to colour and width, should not vary from the patterns and designs given.

KNIGHTS OF THE
ORDER OF POPE ST. SYLVESTER

Their uniform should be of black cloth with coat-tails.

The collar and cuffs should be of black velvet.

A narrow gilt border, decorated with laurel leaves, runs along the top edge and front of the collar, along the top and the side of the cuffs and surrounds the pocket flaps.

There should be nine buttons on the chest and three smaller buttons on each sleeve. The tail of the coat, which borders on the pocket flaps should be adorned with two larger buttons, and in the centre, above the buttons should be two embroidered sprays of laurel leaves in gold thread, arranged in an oval circlet.

The trousers should be long and of black cloth. A gold stripe, decorated with laurel leaves, three centimetres wide, should run down the outer sides of the trousers.

The cocked hat should be of black thick silk. Along the upper rim runs a black silk band to which the Pontifical Cockade is attached on the right side, held by four strands of intertwined gilded cord and fastened at the lower end with a gilded button. A small gold tassel decorates the hat at either end.

The buttons, all gilded, should be embossed with the Cross of the Order. The court sword should be worn in a sword frog, made of gold braid decorated with laurel leaves. The sword should bear on the hilt the Cross of the Order. The handle should be of mother of pearl with gilded mounts and with a gilt sword-knot hanging from it. The scabbard should be of black leather with a gilt boss and ferrule.

The Cross of the Order is an eight-pointed, silver-rimmed white enamel Maltese cross with four clusters of eight shorter gilded rays protruding between the arms of the Cross. In the centre of the Cross is a blue medallion with a silver-rimmed yellow border, bearing in gilt relief the image of Pope St. Sylvester wearing a tiara, and in the yellow border the words SANC SILVESTER P.M.

A Knight of the Order wears the Cross, four centimetres in diameter, on a ribbon, three and a half centimetres wide, of black moiré with three red

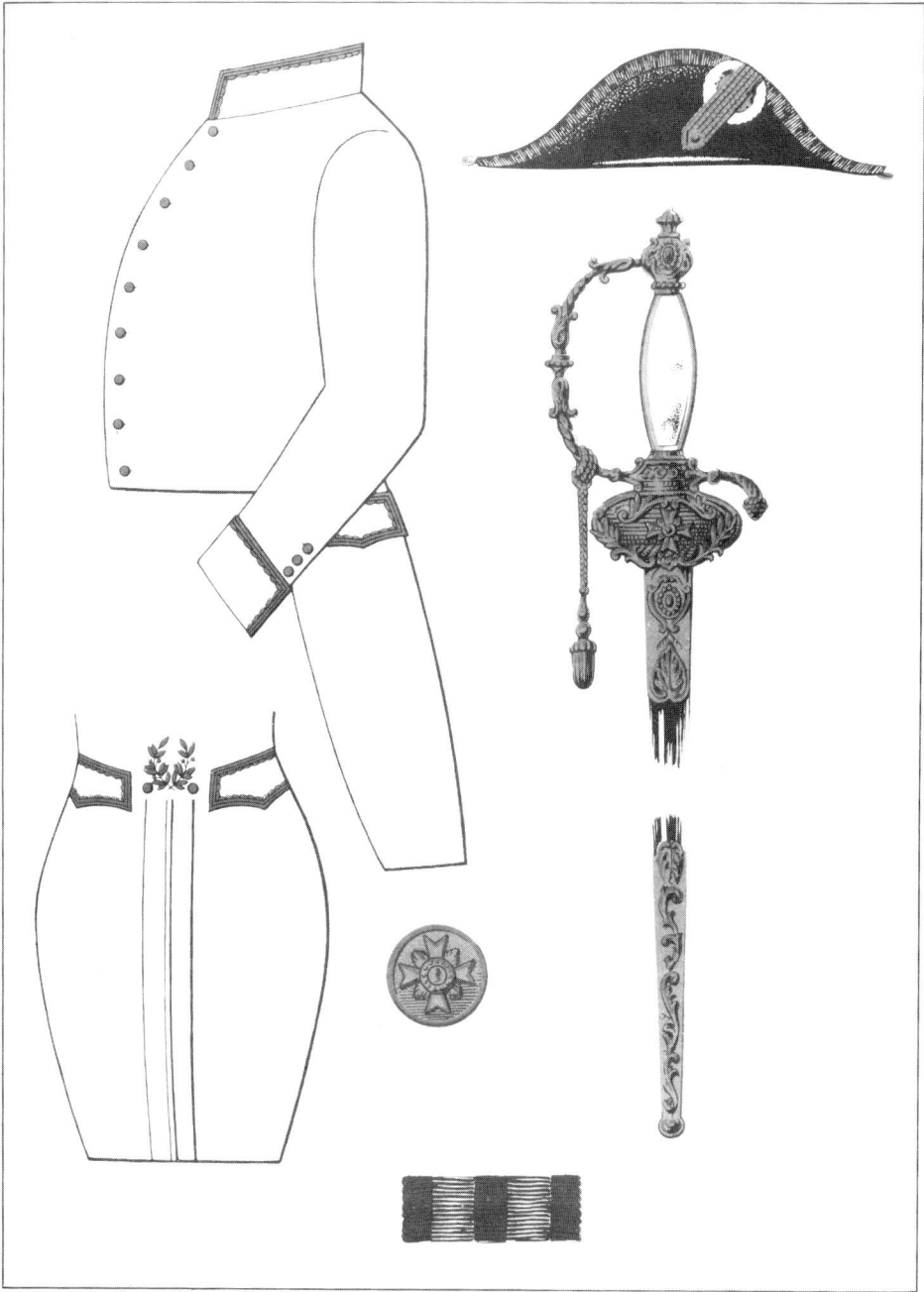

stripes, one in the centre and one at each border, on the left side of his breast.

The Cross and buttons, according to their shape and sizes, and the ribbon, bands and stripes, according to their colour and width, should not vary from the patterns and designs given.

LUIGI CARD. MACCHI
Grand Master of the Pontifical Equestrian Orders

4

ADDITIONAL GUIDELINES TO THE WEARING OF THE UNIFORM OF A PAPAL KNIGHT

Most of the suggestions on matters of dress for Papal Knights which follow have come from Brigadier Gordon Viner, CBE, OBE, MC, KSG, the Honorary Secretary of the Papal Knights in Great Britain. They are practical and helpful suggestions and at the same time a positive step towards greater perfection. All Papal Knights will agree that if something is worth doing, it is worth doing well. Because of the unique status of a Papal Knight, nobody but the Holy Father or the Cardinal Secretary of State can lay down rules and regulations for the correct uniform of a Knight, and that was done last on 7 February 1905 when the Grand Chancellor promulgated the rules on behalf of the Supreme Pontiff, Pope St. Pius X.

However, not only times and values have changed since the beginning of the twentieth century, but more mundane things as well. In 1905, it was taken for granted that a gentleman, an officer, let alone a Knight, would wear white gloves when dressing for festive occasions; he also would wear an appropriate collar. Hence, neither white gloves nor a collar are mentioned in the rules about uniforms for Papal Knights. Similarly, there is no mention about footwear because they too were part of the accepted rules for wearing dress uniforms.

When the rules for the uniforms were published in 1905, gentlemen wore shirts with loose collars and often loose cuffs. The question of a correct collar to be worn under the uniform is not a matter of fashion but a substantial money saver: those who have had their uniform cleaned, know how prohibitively expensive this can be. The uniform collar first indicates the need for having the uniform cleaned; it is approximately 4.5 cm high and specially stiffened. In the case of the Knight wearing a neck badge, it is worn under the collar. In either case, the stiffened collar of the uniform, probably heavily embroidered, or the ribbon of the neck badge will soon feel rather uncomfortable on the neck and possibly cause a rash. In hot or humid conditions the collar will absorb the moisture, and after a while it will not only need cleaning but will have become rather limp. The sleeves do not suffer quite as badly as the collar but a similar effect may be noticed.

All these problems can be solved and much cleaning expense saved by doing what Papal Knights used to do in 1905. They wore a shirt with a loose collar, and before putting the uniform on, affixed a Roman collar (such as are worn by priests) with two studs. One or two of the plastic collars should be acquired, five centimetres high, which allows about five milimetres to show above the uniform collar and enhances the appearance. These can be wiped clean with a damp cloth. Knights wearing a neck badge place the ribbon between the white collar and the uniform collar with the badge or cross protruding above the top button according to the regulations, and they will no longer experience the discomfort on the skin of the neck.

Most cleaning firms offer a tailoring service, and ordinary shirts can be fitted with white cuffs and a white collar rim to hold a loose collar. It makes it possible to have the cuffs specially starched which allows for about one centimetre of the cuffs to show protruding from the sleeves.

Roman collars can be obtained from ecclesiastical tailors, but Knights are advised to acquire collars five centimetres high.

The correct footwear is mess boots which can usually be had in larger shoe shops only.

When travelling by air or abroad, transporting the sword can present problems; airlines, Customs and Police alike consider the sword of a Papal Knight a dangerous weapon. To avoid difficulties it is possible to have a wooden case built, lined with foam rubber which has been cut to the shape of the sword and lined with a soft cloth. The case needs a lock and two additional clasps. If it is carried as hand luggage, one should ask the Airport Security for personal inspection because it causes a panic when put through the x-ray machine. Given in as luggage at the check-in-desk, problems can arise at the Customs or Security Checks abroad especially on the return journey. An appropriate certificate, preferably with a passport-type photograph which has been stamped by the Nunciature, will generally put the mind of the officers at rest.

As to the wearing of Orders and decorations, there are rules and regulations governing the wearing of them at official state functions or in the presence of the Head of State. As most functions of the Papal Knights are religious or private functions, the wearing of decorations which because of

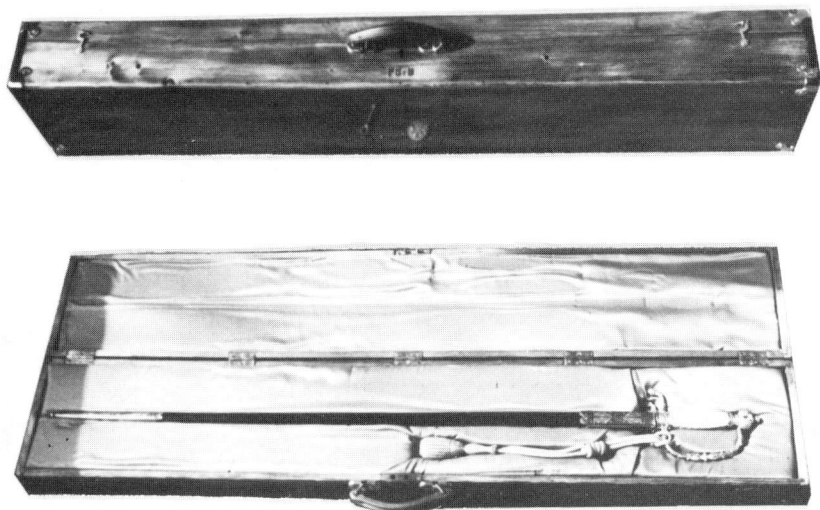

This sword travelling case was made by a carpenter from pinewood, 1 cm thick, which was later stained dark. The eight corners of the case are strengthened with steel corners and a handle fitted above a lock; left and right a catch to secure the closed case. It is lined with foam rubber; the bottom layer has the shape of the hilt and the sword cut out before the foam rubber is lined with cloth. Over-all dimension of closed case: 103 cm x 18 cm x 10 cm deep; weight with sword: 4 kg.

certain regulations have not as yet received the Monarch's unrestricted permission to be worn, those of the Sovereign Military of Malta, the Equestrian Order of the Holy Sepulchre of Jerusalem or the S.M. Constantinian Order of St. George, is a matter of personal choice*, but Brigadier Viner points out that all Orders, those of the State, followed by those with permission of the Head of State to be worn, should be on one bar. Only decorations which by statute are worn on the right breast should be worn there and not those which are normally worn on the left. As far as private or religious functions of Papal Knights are concerned, only those Orders or Awards which have been expressly approved by the Holy See may be worn with the uniform. According to several Papal Briefs, decorations of self-styled Orders may not be worn.

* Special attention is drawn to Part III, the last paragraph on *The Most Venerable Order of St. John of Jerusalem*, a Royal Order, of which H.M. the Queen is the Sovereign Head and H.R.H. The Duke of Gloucester Grand Prior. Although the Queen's regulations concerning the wearing of decorations are strictly enforced by the Order, an exception is expressly made for Knights of the Sovereign Military Order of Malta and those upon whom has been conferred the Order *Pro Merito Melitensi*, who may wear their insignia at social and religious functions of the Most Venerable Order of St. John.

Some duties at the Papal Court were the prerogatives of Papal Chamberlains; they would meet and accompany newly accredited ambassadors to the Holy See when they arrived at the Apostolic Palace to present their credentials, (left and centre). Nowadays one sees frequently a Gentleman-in-Waiting to His Holiness in the uniform of a Papal Knight carry out such duties. (Right) A Knight Commander of the Pontifical Equestrian Order of St. Gregory the Great leads an ambassador to his audience with the Pope.

CHAPTER FOUR

CONFERMENT OF INSIGNIA AND INVESTITURE OF A PAPAL KNIGHT

The difference between a conferment and an investiture can be defined linguistically. An honour, title or decoration is conferred by giving it to the recipient together with a document of conferment. Investing a person implies that the candidate is robed with a garment or insignia and endowed with quality, office or rank.

As the insignia of the Pontifical Equestrian Orders compromise the Cross and the uniform, a candidate can be invested either in the true meaning of the word, or symbolically, when the conferment of the Cross is the visible part of the investiture, and the commitment made by the newly invested Knight in response to the Bishop's request represents the spiritual mantle with which he is robed by the Bishop.

Medieval customs during an investiture, such as the dubbing of a Knight, are no longer part of the procedure for Pontifical Equestrian Orders. However, Catholics and non-Catholics upon whom a Papal Knighthood is conferred are no less deserving of recognition, nor are their services less appreciated, than those who are invested.

Any Catholic Papal Knight upon whom a decoration has been conferred can arrange with his Local Bishop and Parish Priest to be invested during the celebration of the Eucharist.

Many Papal Knights have the decoration conferred on them because it is the only practical way in which it can be done at the time. For example, those working in the Vatican who receive a Papal Knighthood have it usually conferred on them by a Curial Cardinal; such a Conferment usually takes place during an audience or on a special occasion.

Gentlemen living abroad who have been honoured with a Papal Knighthood *motu proprio* will have it conferred by the Apostolic Nuncio, who will present to them the decoration and the Papal Brief.

Papal Knighthoods are occasionally conferred during an audience with the Holy Father. According to tradition and custom, the Pope does not decorate the candidate himself; if for personal or other reasons the procedure of sending the decoration in advance of the audience is waived, the Pope may hand the decoration to the candidate, but the Prefect of the Pontifical Household or another high dignitary present will decorate the recipient.

In the Vatican a Knighthood is usually conferred on a candidate by one of the Cardinals of the Curia. On 9 November 1986, His Eminence Edouard Cardinal Gagnon conferred the dignity of a Knight Commander of the Pontifical Equestrian Order of St. Gregory the Great on Mr. Pierre Blanchard of the Administration of the Patrimony of the Holy See.

Such occasions are usually restricted to an honour that has been granted *motu proprio* by the Pope and to persons who have given exceptionally meritorious service to the Holy Father.

The Supreme Order of Christ is usually conferred personally by the Supreme Pontiff on Roman Catholic Monarchs and, occasionally, on a Catholic Head of State. This is a very rare honour. Catholic Sovereigns or Heads of State receive more often the Order of the Golden Spur or the Golden Collar of the Pian Order. Non-Catholic but Christian Monarchs and Heads of State are also eligible for the Order of the Golden Spur; non-Christian Monarchs or Heads of State are eligible for the Golden Collar of the Pian Order. Pope Paul VI made this ruling in his Papal Brief *De Ordinum Equestrium*, dated 15 April 1966. The protocol governing the conferment of Orders for Heads of State has also been relaxed, and it is not uncommon for the Supreme Pontiff to hand the decoration to the recipient during an audience instead of having the decoration delivered to the recipient's residence just prior to it. It now varies from occasion to occasion.

The following are the criteria for the bestowal of the other Pontifical Orders of Knighthood:

THE ORDER OF PIUS IX, was founded in 1847 by Pope Pius IX to reward conspicuous deeds of merit in Church and society, and otherwise known as the Pian Order, is today conferred mainly on diplomats accredited to the Holy See, visiting statesmen or personal representatives of Sovereigns or Heads of States, or for personal services rendered to the Pope.

THE ORDER OF ST. GREGORY THE GREAT, was founded in 1831 by Pope Gregory XVI; it is conferred as a reward for services to the Holy See on gentlemen of proved loyalty who must maintain unswerving fidelity to God, the Sovereign Pontiff, the Holy See and the Holy Church.

THE ORDER OF POPE ST. SYLVESTER, founded in 1841 by Pope Gregory XVI to absorb the Order of the Golden Spur, and made a separate Order in 1905 by Pope St. Pius X, is conferred on laymen who are active in the apostolate, particularly in the exercise of their professional duties, and who are masters of different arts.

The latter is frequently conferred on non-Catholics and non-Christians. Eminent professional men, such as physicians, surgeons, lawyers and scientists of many religious faiths have received the Order, as have artists, musicians, and gentlemen in the film industry, the press and television.

The criterion ". . . who are active in the apostolate" stresses the leadership of a person in his particular field of activity; it can also refer to the work of a Catholic in a specific apostolate of the Church.

Catholics who are invested with the insignia of a Pontifical Equestrian Order during or after the celebration of the Eucharist promise the Bishop who conducts the investiture: "faithfully to maintain unswerving fidelity to God and the Supreme Pontiff, to the Holy See and the Church".

Although these are the particular criteria for being created a Knight of the Order of St. Gregory the Great, the promise is the commitment all Catholic Knights make when they are invested during a Holy Mass, whatever Order they are appointed to. It is the spiritual mantle they take upon themselves.

INVESTITURE
of
NICOLA VECCHIONE, Esq.

AS A KNIGHT OF THE PONTIFICAL EQUESTRIAN
ORDER OF ST. GREGORY THE GREAT

BY

RIGHT REVEREND MGR. GERALD MAHON
BISHOP IN WEST LONDON

on SUNDAY, 1 FEBRUARY, 1987
DURING PONTIFICAL HIGH MASS
at 10 a.m.

IN THE PARISH CHURCH
OF THE MOST SACRED HEART
RUISLIP, MIDDLESEX

CONCELEBRANT: THE PARISH PRIEST,
REV. ADRIAN ARROWSMITH

CHAPTER FIVE

INVESTITURE OF A PAPAL KNIGHT
BY THE LOCAL BISHOP
IN THE KNIGHT'S PARISH CHURCH

When an investiture of a Papal Knight takes place in the Parish Church of a newly appointed Knight, the Bishop who will conduct the ceremony will do so during the celebration of Holy Mass or, after the celebration of the Eucharist, in a Church Hall.

The actual pcocedure of investiture is the same for all Catholic Knights; what can differ is the scale on which an investiture is planned if, for example, it takes place in a Cathedral. Wherever a Papal Knight is invested, the main aim of the organisers should be to highlight the dignity and importance of the occasion.

Much of what applies to an investiture in a Parish Church applies equally to such a ceremony in a Cathedral. The procedures which have been compiled here are guidelines and not inflexible rules.

1.

PREPARATIONS FOR THE INVESTITURE

It is very exceptional that a newly appointed Knight has acquired a uniform before the investiture, which makes it even more desirable that one or more Papal Knights in uniform should be in attendance. This not only demonstrates the ceremonial function and one of the privileges a Papal Knight enjoys, namely to be in attendance on ecclesiastical dignitaries, but also the *esprit de corps* of the Papal Knights who welcome the new confrère into the midst of the chivalric fraternity.

If the candidate for investiture has been appointed to the Equestrian Order of St. Gregory the Great, a uniformed Knight of that Order should be present; if the candidate is to be invested with the insignia of the Equestrian Order of Pope St. Sylvester, a uniformed member of that Order should be present if possible. However, because of the closeness with which the Pontifical Equestrian Orders work together, Knights in uniform of either or both Orders should endeavour to be present.

If more than one uniformed Pontifical Knight takes part, the Knight who will assist the Bishop during the investiture is for the sake of clarity here referred to as the Sponsor. If it proves impossible to have a Knight in uniform present, the Master of Ceremonies can undertake the function of the Sponsor.

A Knight is invested in a Pontifical Order only once; should he be promoted within the Order at a later time, it is more appropriate to follow a different procedure. Of course, those who are promoted from Knight to Knight Commander, or from Knight Commander to Knight Grand Cross, may wish to celebrate the occasion with the celebration of the Eucharist. The most suitable place for receiving the new insignia would be at the Bishop's residence after the Eucharist.

Once a Knight has been invested in a Pontifical Order of Knighthood and promised his fidelity to God, the Supreme Pontiff, the Holy See and the Church, there is no need to repeat this promise on promotion. Conferment of a rank in another Pontifical Order of Knighthood at a later time is also regarded as a promotion and no new investiture is necessary.

If a Knight has received his decoration during a ceremony of conferment, he can still have an investiture during the celebration of Holy Mass. He is advised to speak to his Local Bishop and Parish Priest about such an arrangement.

An investiture in the Knight's Parish Church is no less of an important event than one held in a Cathedral. On the contrary, it affords the entire parish family to witness a rare pontifical occasion.

An investiture in a Parish Church needs close cooperation between the Parish Priest and his Master of Ceremonies. This applies not only to procedure and preparations of special facilities, but specially to matters which, if they are overlooked, can ruin the best prepared ceremony.

Any investiture or conferment of a cross or medal needs close attention to detail. It is necessary to check, for example, the Cross or Medal which is to be conferred, especially the mechanism with which the decoration is fastened onto the left breast of the recipient. If it is faulty, it is too late to repair it during the ceremony. Anybody about to receive a papal decoration should be told in advance that the cross or medal will be fastened to the breast pocket (or in the case of a lady receiving an award, to the dress) so that the recipient can make provision to prevent damage to the suit.

This can easily be done by fastening two safety pins vertically, three centimetres apart, from the inside of the garment, leaving two small loops next to each other through which the usually thick pin of the cross or medal can be slipped horizontally. Special care must be taken when a star of an Order is conferred. Many stars are fastened with thick vertical pins and sometimes narrow bars. If the recipient of a star is not in uniform, the thick pin or bar can be slipped into the breast pocket of the suit; if, however, the star is to be fastened to an uniform or morning dress, a similiar provision can be made by the recipient with two safety pins from the inside of the jacket, placed horizonally, about five centimetres above each other, to allow the thick pin or bar to be slipped vertically through the two loops.

After the Bishop and Parish Priest have arranged the date and time of the Holy Mass during which the invesiture will take place, the Bishop will ask the Hon. Secretary of the local or national Association of Papal Knights if it is possible for a Papal Knight in uniform to assist during the investiture. Also, most Associations have lists of members available which indicate who has a uniform. A Bishop may have Papal Knights in uniform in his diocese and he could get in touch with them directly. An updated list of Papal Knights can usually be had from the Secretary of the national Association.˙

If more than one Knight in uniform can attend the function, it highlights the importance of the occasion. The main function of Papal Knights in uniform is to be in attendance upon the Bishop and other ecclesiastical dignitaries; Papal Knights form with the Bishop's Secretary and ecclesiastical attendants the episcopal curia at the ceremony.

The Bishop processes into the Church, flanked by the concelebrating Deacon and Subdeacon, or by the Parish Priest and his Chaplain. The Sponsor will walk behind the Bishop, bringing the procession to a close. If more uniformed Papal Knights are present, they walk either immediately in front of the Bishop or, if other Bishops or high Prelates are in the procession, those Knights will be in attendance upon them, walking in front of the Prelates.

If members of other Chivalric Orders attend in their robes, such as the Order of the Holy Sepulchre of Jerusalem, of which many Knights are also Papal Knights, they will enter the Church in a separate procession. They take their allocated seats approximately five minutes before the main procession enters; a verger or senior server should be available to lead the Knights and Dames to their seats.

A gentleman or lady usher to look after the seats that have been reserved in the front of the church, can avoid the embarrassment to have to ask parishioners to move to a seat further back. A small incident like finding reserved seats occupied when the procession enters, can cause delays and hold-ups. It can disturb the dignity of an occasion.

Papal Knights of the Parish who are not in uniform and parishioners who have been honoured with a Papal Award of Merit should also attend the

---

* The Hon. Secretary for the Papal Knights in Great Britain can always be found in the *Catholic Directory*, published annually on behalf of the Hierarchy by the *The Universe*.

fuction; they should wear either morning dress or a dark lounge suit with the full-size decoration of a Papal Knight. A Knight Commander should wear his Cross on a neck riband, the laurel wreath above the Cross should rest immediately under the knot of his tie. One Star, where appropriate, may also worn on morning dress or lounge suit, but no sash of a Grand Cross. Parishioners who are holders of a Pontifical Award, the *Pro Ecclesia et Pontifice* or *Benemerenti*, should also wear their full-size decoration. They should be allocated their places in the front rows opposite the candidate for investitute. Special arrangements may have to be made if civic dignitaries attend the ceremony. In such an event it would be appropriate to have an uniformed Knight in attendance upon the civic dignitaries, receiving them at the entrance, taking them to their places and leading them out after the service, following directly behind the Bishop's procession.

When the main procession reaches the altar, the Sponsor takes his place near the Bishop, where a seat and a kneeler are provided for him. If more Papal Knights in uniform are present, seats and kneelers should be made available to them as well.

Such arrangements are flexible and should be suited to the lay-out of the church. A few minutes of a personal discussion concerning the arrangements, procession and allocation of seats, between the Parish Priest, Master of Ceremonies, some of the senior servers, the Sponsor and the Knight to be invested, achieve usually more than ten books of instructions.

The Sponsor assists the Bishop only during the actual investiture; he will remain at his place throughout the Eucharist. However, other Papal Knights could be given special tasks, such as reading the lesson or taking the offerings to the Celebrant.

Arrangements should be made in advance with the Parish Priest if the Papal Knights will take Holy Communion; a server may be given the task of taking them to a pre-arranged place.

It is at the discretion of the Parish Priest at what moment during the Holy Mass the invesiture will take place. He will discuss this with his Bishop and make the initial plans with his Master of Ceremonies; details can be discussed at a meeting with the other active participants nearer to the actual event.

Whenever possible, the Mass of St. Gregory the Great or at St. Silvester should be celebrated.

The ceremony of investiture should take place before the final Blessing by the Bishop. Most Parish Priests and also Bishops favour it immediately following the Gospel.

The candidate for the investiture should be seated at the front by the centre aisle. If only one candidate is to be invested, it would be appropriate to make arrangments for his famiy to be seated with him. If there are more candidates for investiture, they should be seated in the order in which they are to be invested, and arrangements should be made to have the families seated near the candidates.

At the pre-arranged time during the Mass, the Bishop will ask the Sponsor or the Master of Ceremonies to bring before him the candidate to be invested.

2.

THE INVESTITURE

The Cross which will be conferred on the Knight and the Papal Brief have been placed in advance on the right side of the altar.

The Bishop will rise, turn to the Sponsor and say:

"Let the candidate for investiture into the Order of St. Gregory the Great [or: *the Order of Pope St. Sylvester*] be brought forward."

The Sponsor will walk towards the candidate. At the same time,servers bearing mitre and crozier take them to the Bishop who takes up his position in front of the altar so that the investiture can take place in full view of the congregation. The mitred Bishop stands in the centre, the Parish Priest and other concelebrants on either side of him. The Master of Ceremonies and the servers in the entourage take up positions left and right on the lower steps, facing each other, but making sure that ample room remains for the investiture to be seen by the congregation.

The candidate rises as the Sponsor approaches and then walks on his left side towards the Bishop. Three steps in front of the Bishop both will halt, bow, and the Sponsor will address the Bishop:

"My Lord Bishop

I have the honour of presenting to you

....

to be invested with the insignia of a

....

of the Pontifical Equestrian Order of

St. Gregory the Great."
(or: St. Sylvester"

The Parish Priest of the Candidate for the investiture, Fr. Adrian Arrowsmith, led the Right Reverend Mgr. Gerald Mahon, Bishop in West London, who conducted the ceremony, in procession to the church. The Candidate's Sponsor in the Pontifical Equestrian Order of St. Gregory the Great, a Knight Commander of the Order, was in attendance upon, and walked behind the Bishop, who concelebrated the Pontifical High Mass with the Parish Priest.

(Opposite above)
An investiture in a Parish Church not only allows its members to attend a rare pontifical function, but the emphasis of the celebration is on the family. The candidate to be invested as a Papal Knight, Mr. Nicola Vecchione, had taken his place on the Gospel side of the nave, next to the centre aisle. With him were his wife, two sons and daughter, and in the pews behind him, his mother and other members of his family. Well over a thousand parishioners attended the Pontifical High Mass. A programme of the investiture ceremony had been prepared by the Master of Ceremonies which allowed those present to follow the procedure.

(Opposite below)
An investiture allows the Parish to honour also those who have on earlier occasions received a Papal Knighthood or an Award of Merit. Two Knights of the Pontifical Equestrian Order of St. Gregory the Great, and eight parishioners who had received the Papal Awards Pro Ecclesia et Pontifice or the Medal Benemerenti took their places in the three front rows on the Epistle side of the nave. All wore their decorations.

76

For the investiture the Mass of St. Gregory the Great was celebrated. After the reading of the Gospel, the Bishop, wearing mitre and crozier, and the Parish Priest, accompanied by the Master of Ceremonies, processed to the front of the altar. Throughout the Mass the Candidate's Sponsor had remained at his *prie-dieu* (visible in the front right of the picture). The Bishop asked the Sponsor to present the Candidate, and both approached the altar for the investiture ceremony.

The Bishop now addresses the newly appointed Knight and the Congregation:

> "The Pontifical Order of St. Gregory the Great was founded in 1831 by Pope Gregory XVI. It is conferred as a reward for services to the Holy See and the Church on gentlemen of proved loyalty who must maintain unswerving fidelity to God, the Supreme Pontiff, the Holy See and the Church.

or, if the Knight is proposed to be invested with the insignia of the Order of Pope St. Silvester:

> "The Pontifical Order of Pope St. Sylvester was founded in 1841 by Pope Gregory XVI. The Order is conferred on laymen who are active in the apostolate, particularly in the exercise of their professional duties, and on those who are masters of the different arts.

> "The Papal Secretary of State, has defined the rôle of a Papal Knight:

'Becoming a Knight does not merely mean receiving a title of honour — even though it is well deserved — but fighting evil, promoting good, and defending the weak and oppressed against injustice'.

"The Papal Brief which creates you a .... of the Pontifical Order of St. Gregory the Great [or of Pope St. Sylvester] reads as follows:

JOANNES PAULUS SECUNDUS PONTIFEX MAXIMUS

JOHN PAUL II SUPREME PONTIFF

Gladly acceding to a request made to Us from which we have gathered that you are most deserving for what you have done for the Holy Catholic Church and its affairs, and in order that We might give a clear sign of Our pleasure and appreciation, We choose, make and declare you

....

of the Diocese of ....

a .... of the Order of St.

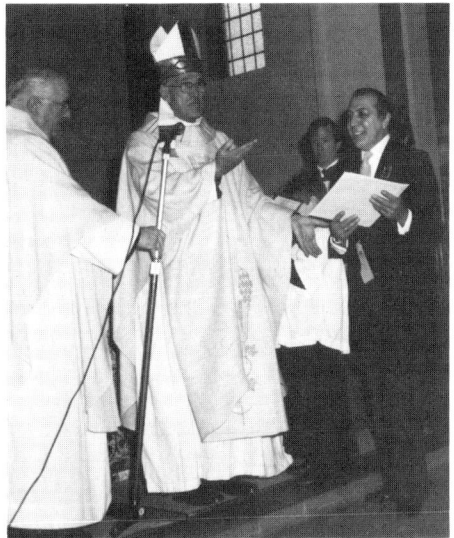

(Left) Right Reverend Bishop Mahon conferred the Cross of a Knight of the Pontifical Equestrian Order of St. Gregory the Great on Mr. Nicola Vecchione, and (right) he handed him the Papal Brief which created him a Knight. After the service, he received the statutes of the Order and the box for the insignia.

Gregory the Great [or Pope St. Sylvester] We bestow on you the right to use and enjoy all the privileges which go with this high dignity.

Given at St. Peter's in Rome on ....

Signed and sealed by the Cardinal Secretary of State

If more candidates are to be invested, the Bishop will read the different Papal Briefs.

The Bishop continues:

"I have been delegated by His Holines Pope John Paul II to invest you with the insignia of the Order to which He has appointed you.

"Before performing this solemn task, I must ask you: Do you promise faithfully to maintain unswerving fidelity to God, the Supreme Pontiff, the Holy See and to the Holy Church and exercise the office of a Pontifical Knight in accordance with the high ideals and standards expected of you?"

The candidate replies:
"I promise so to do!"

The Bishop:
"Please step forward!"

The candidate steps forward towards the Bishop. The Sponsor also ascends the steps and takes the Cross and the Papal Brief from the altar, taking his position on the right side of the candidate.

The Bishop continues in the meantime:

"In the name of the Holy Father I herewith invest you with the insignia of a .... of the Pontifical Order of St. Gregory the Great [or of Pope St. Sylvester] and I present to you the Papal Brief."

The Sponsor now hands the Cross to the Bishop who will affix a Cross of a Knight onto the left breast pocket of the candidate or decorate a Knight Commander with the neck badge. The Sponsor then hands the Papal Brief to the Bishop who presents it to the new Knight.

The Sponsor and the new Knight will step back to the bottom step. Together they bow to the Bishop, make a right turn, and the Sponsor will lead the new Knight to his seat, and then return to his place.

The Bishop and his entourage return to their places while the new Knight is led to his place.

After the celebration of the Eucharist, Bishop Mahon (with the two acolytes who carried the Bishop's crozier and mitre during the service) and the Parish Priest, Fr. Adrian Arrowsmith, accompanied Mr. Nicola Vecchione, K.S.G., to the Church Hall, where the parishioners had gathered to congratulate the new Knight on the high honour the Supreme Pontiff had bestowed on him.

This is the end of the Investiture.

The address by the Bishop or Parish Priest follows now.

[If it is the wish of the newly invested Knight to express his gratitude to the Holy Father, the Bishop and the Parish Priest, the Knight may do so after the post-communion prayers have been said. Before the concluding prayer of the Mass, the Parish Priest will invite him to come forward to a pre-arranged place from where the Knight will speak.]

3.

CONFERMENT OF PONTIFICAL AWARDS
PRO ECCLESIA ET PONTIFICE
and *BENEMERENTI*

Both Pontifical Awards have pontifical status and their rightful place among Awards of Merit in the international family of decorations.

It is appropriate to outline a possible procedure for the conferment of Papal Awards similar to that for Papal Knighthoods because the services of the recipients to the Church and community are highly recognised. In a parish family the conferment of Papal Awards is an important event, and the procedure of conferment could follow a similar pattern to the invesiture of a Knight.

If at a service of investiture of a Knight, the conferment of either of the two Pontifical Awards were to take place, they should follow immediately the investiture.

The Bishop may confer the Awards himself or delegate the task of representing the Holy Father to the Parish Priest.

After the newly invested Knight has returned to his seat, the Bishop or the Parish Priest (Conferrer) will ask the Master of Ceremonies:

'Please bring those to me upon whom the Holy Father has conferred a Pontifical Award of Merit."

The recipient(s) will also be seated at the front of the Church, and the Master of Ceremonies will bring them before the Conferrer who will now address the recipient(s) and the Congregation:

(either)

"The Cross *PRO ECCLESIA ET PONTIFICE* (for Church and Pontiff) was instituted by Pope Leo XIII in 1888 to mark the occasion of his priestly golden jubilee. It is awarded to men and women as a sign of the Supreme Pontiff's recognition of their distinugished service to the Church and society".

(or/and)

"A *BENEMERENTI* Medal was first awarded by Pope Pius IV in 1775. Similar medals have continued to be bestowed on men and women distinguishing themselves for their special service or accomplishment. In 1891 Pope Leo XIII instituted the *BENEMERENTI* Medal as a permanent Award of Merit. In 1971 Pope Paul VI changed the *BENEMERENTI* Medal to a Cross. It is awarded to men and women who have rendered significant service to the Church and society."

The Conferrer now reads the Apostolic Diploma conferring the Cross *Pro Ecclesia et Pontifice* or the Award Benemerenti:

JOANNES PAULUS SECUNDUS PONTIFEX MAXIMUS
JOHN PAUL II, SUPREME PONTIFF

Gladly acceding to a request made to Us from which We have discerned that you are most deserving for all that you have done for the Church

In June 1987, three members of the Parish Church of the Most Sacred Heart in Ruislip, Middlesex, received the Papal Award *Pro Ecclesia et Pontifice* from Right Reverend Mgr. Mahon, Bishop in West London. (Above) Nicola Vecchione, K.S.G., who was invested here as a Knight of the Order of St. Gregory the Great in February, acted as the Sponsor of the three candidates and presented them to the Bishop, (left) who conferred the Award.

and the Holy Father, and as a clear sign of Our pleasure, We award you the decoration:

THE CROSS *PRO ECCLESIA ET PONTIFICE*
(or THE MEDAL *BENEMERENTI*)

Given at the Vatican

....

Sostituto

The Awards of Merit and the Apostolic Diplomas have been placed in advance on the right side of the altar. The Master of Ceremonies takes the appropriate Award and Papal Brief, while the Conferrer asks the recipient to step forward and says:

"On behalf of the Holy Father I confer on you the Papal Award of Merit *'Pro Ecclesia et Pontifice'* (or *Benemerenti*) and present to you the Apostolic Diploma."

The Master of Ceremonies hands to the Conferrer the Award which is fastened on the left side of the breast, and then the Apostolic Diploma, which the Conferrer gives to the recipient.

The conferment of the Award(s) of Merit having been concluded, the Master of Ceremonies will take the recipient(s) back to their places.

The address by the Bishop or Parish Priest mentioned above after the conclusion of the investiture of a Knight, will be given now.

This procedure can be followed if there has been no investiture of a Papal Knight. However, if the Parish has a Papal Knight in uniform, he would, no doubt, be happy to exercise the privilege he enjoys and undertake ceremonial duties, attend upon the Bishop and assist with the conferment of Papal Awards.

4.

INVESTITURE OF A PAPAL KNIGHT
IN THE PARISH HALL

There may be reasons why an investiture should take place after the Eucharist. In this case those invited to attend, will assemble in the Church Hall.

The same procedure of investiture as is used during Holy Mass can be used in a Parish Hall with minor omissions. However, it should take place before drinks and refreshments are offered to the guests.

An appropriate area should be kept clear for the Bishop and his entourage.

When the guests are assembled, the Master of Ceremonies leads the Bishop, the Parish Priest, Clergy, the Sponsor and the candidate for investiture to the allocated places.

The Bishop and the Parish Priest will step onto a rostrum (if there is one) and face the guests. The Sponsor and the candidate for investiture will stand facing the Bishop.

The Bishop begins with the words:

"Will the Knight upon whom the insignia of a .... of the Pontifical Equestrian Order of St. Gregory the Great [or: of Pope St. Sylvester] are to be conferred, please step forward".

The candidate and the Sponsor who carries the Cross and the Papal Brief will walk up to the Bishop and bow. (In the absence of a Papal Knight in uniform), the Master of Ceremonies can carry out the function of assisting the Bishop during the investiture).

If more than one Knight is to be invested, the Bishop will ask the candidates to step forward individually, and if ranks or Orders differ, take this into account when inviting them to be invested.

The Bishop continues:

"The Pontifical Order of St. Gregory the Great [or: of Pope St. Sylvester] was founded ....etc."

The Sponsor will hand the Cross and the Papal Brief to the Bishop at the appropriate time.

After the Bishop has completed the investiture, both Knights will bow to the Bishop and return to the Hall.

If a conferment of Papal Awards takes place, the Bishop or the Parish Priest will now ask the recipient(s) to come forward.

The Conferrer begins with the reading of the criteria for granting the Award. The Master of Ceremonies will hand to the Conferrer the Cross or Medal and, after it has been conferred, the Apostolic Diploma. The recipient(s) will bow and return to the Hall. The Parish Priest will announce the end of the formal proceedings, when refreshments can be served.

INVESTITURE
of
TERENCE CASEY, ESQ., C.B.E.

AS A KNIGHT OF THE PONTIFICAL EQUESTRIAN ORDER OF ST. GREGORY THE GREAT

BY

RIGHT REVEREND MGR. JAMES HANNIGAN BISHOP OF MENEVIA

AT

WESTMINSTER CATHEDRAL

DURING CAPITULAR MASS

on THURSDAY, 26 FEBRUARY, 1987 at 5.30 p.m.

INVESTITURE OF A PAPAL KNIGHT BY AN ARCHBISHOP OR THE DIOCESAN BISHOP IN THE CATHEDRAL DURING THE CELEBRATON OF HOLY MASS

A newly appointed Knight will be invested in the Cathedral either during a Pontifical High Mass, a Capitular Mass or a Special Eucharist for the occasion.

1.

PREPARATION FOR AN INVESTITURE

The Priest responsible for religious functions in a Cathedral is the Administrator, who is the Parish Priest of the Cathedral. He consults with the Master of Ceremonies of the Diocese with regard to all matters of religious services in the Cathedral.

The preparations for an investiture in a Cathedral are the same as for those in a Parish Church, though the organisation will be on a larger scale. The Administrator of the Cathedral will liaise with the Hon. Secretary of the Papal Knights for an appropriate number of Papal Knights in uniform to attend the investiture, and he will, if possible, arrange a joint meeting with the Master of Ceremonies and the Knight who will assist the Bishop during the investiture (the Sponsor) to discuss the ceremony. If the Chaplain to the Papal Knights is present, it would be appropriate for him to assist the Bishop during the investiture.

The Administrator may wish to invite Knights and Dames of other Catholic Orders of Chivalry to attend the Mass.

The number of uniformed Papal Knights who take part in the ceremony depends on several circumstances. Apart from the Sponsor, other Papal Knights may be assigned ceremonial or liturgical functions during the Eucharist, such as reading the lesson or taking the offerings to the Celebrant.

The candidates to be invested (and those who receive a Papal Award of Merit after the investiture of Knights) will be seated at the front.

The Master of Ceremonies will have to know the actual number in each of the groups who will attend. He also should be acquainted with any special needs of candidates or guests. Such information should be communicated to the Administrator. It is important to inform the Administrator of the number of guests for whom seats must be reserved.

To avoid a breakdown in communication, all requests or important information should be sent to the Administrator of the Cathedral, clearly indicating to which event (day, month and time) the letter refers. For example, if a person in a wheelchair will be present, whether a recipient of an honour or a guest, the Administrator should be informed as soon as possible to help him make the necessary arrangements.

A room should be set aside for the Papal Knights and also for the other Knights who have been invited to change into their uniforms or robes.

Pontifical Knights have a special place in papal *cortège*; it follows therefore that their place is in the episcopal *cortège*. As is shown elsewhere, in the context of religious services, they must not involve themselves with questions of precedence between chivalric Orders.

The rôle of a Papal Knight is to be in attendance on, serve and protect the person of the Vicar of Christ on Earth and the successors of the Apostles. This is reflected in the tasks assigned to them by Pope St. Pius X and their place in the papal *cortège*. It should also be reflected in the ceremonial tasks assigned to them in processions and during religious services by the Masters of Ceremonies.

From the moment the ceremony gets under way, the Master of Ceremonies is in over-all charge.

About ten minutes before the Bishop's procession enters the Cathedral, the robed Knights and Dames of other Orders, attending as confraternal guests of the Papal Knights, should be led to their seats by a Papal Knight.

It is impossible to lay down rules for a precise time table; unless all the factors are known and can be taken into account, such as the distance the Knights have to walk, and the time it takes them to occupy their seats, the Master of Ceremonies cannot work out any time-table. The saying about the speed of a convoy being that of its slowest ship, applies especially to processions.

A Master of Ceremonies will always wait until all participants are present before deciding on the interval of time between the different groups leaving the sacristy for the Cathedral. He is used to making *ad hoc* decisions and dealing with unforeseen situations. If everything could be run by the instruction book, no Master of Ceremonies would be needed.

It is the task of a Master of Ceremonies to ensure the smooth running of ceremonies, but he can only do so when he knows all the facts and is assured of the cooperation of all the participants.

There have never been any guidelines for the investiture of a Pontifical

Knight, nor can I refer to official precedents. The responsibility for organising an investiture has always rested on the Masters of Ceremonies of Cathedrals or Parish Churches. On many occasions one of the Papal Knights present has taken on the responsibility for arranging a ceremony or used his initiative to do what he felt the occasion demanded.

No book of guidelines can deal with every possible situation: the initiative of the Master of Ceremonies and of the Papal Knight who assists the Bishop with the investiture is the only guarantee of a smooth-running and dignified ceremony.

The position of the Papal Knights in the Bishop's procession and their functions during the Mass depends on the number of uniformed Papal Knights attending the service and on the number of ecclesiastical dignitaries to whom Papal Knights are assigned.

One can only give a broad guideline; in the final analysis common sense must prevail and the Master of Ceremonies of the Cathedral must make the decisions best suited to the occasion. He is in over-all charge.

If the procedure for an investiture of a Papal Knight is adopted, (without sacrificing local customs or traditions built up over the decades), the rôle of the Papal Knights in uniform who are present, especially the tasks of the Sponsor, are clearly defined, and the difficult task of the Master of Ceremonies will be made a little easier. These guidelines will enable all Papal Knights to be familiar with the basic procedure and make it possible for any Papal Knight to act as a Sponsor at an investiture. He would know what his tasks are and take on this rôle with confidence.

For an investiture in a Cathedral, it is essential that everybody knows that the Administrator is in charge of the preparations and facilities and the Master of Ceremonies of the ceremony from the moment the participants gather for the service. The most important part of such a ceremony is the close cooperation between the organising parties and communication between all parties concerned.

There is one precedent which could serve with regard to the number of Papal Knights in attendance on high dignitaries. While retaining the Swiss Guard and increasing their number and duties, Pope Paul VI abolished the other ceremonial Guards who had always attended pontifical and often international religious occasions.

Papal Knights have been more and more frequently called upon to attend on cardinals and other members of the Roman Curia on special occasions. Their function is not the same as those of the Swiss Guard, but it would be wrong to think that their presence is just oranamental. Naturally, a Pontifical Knight in his splendid uniform will add to the festive look of a Cardinal's or Bishop's *cortège*.

On great occasions, especially when the Holy Father has appointed a Papal Legate to represent him at an Eucharistic Congress, a special pilgrimage or a festival at a Holy Shrine, Papal Knights have an important rôle to play. It is a most difficult task to organise the attendance of Papal Knights on an international basis, and often it has been due to the initiative of individual Knights who attended a congress or pilgrimage, that the Papal Legate and Cardinals received the honours due to them. Where functions have been organised jointly by the national or local Association of Papal Knights, the Master of Ceremonies of the Cathedral where the ceremony took place and the Secretary of the Local Bishops Conference, some practices have evolved which can serve as useful precedents.

Providing sufficient Papal Knights in uniform can attend a function, then, as a general rule, a Papal Legate, Cardinals, the Apostolic Nuncio and Archbishops are each assigned two Papal Knights. However, to lay down such a rule is like legislating on the length of a piece of string.

If sufficient Papal Knights in uniform can attend an investiture, the Bishop who conducts the ceremony in a Cathedral (this could be a Cardinal, the Apostolic Nuncio, the Metropolitan, the Diocesan Bishop, a Bishop specially delegated to invest the Knight or an auxiliary Bishop), should have two Papal Knights in attendance in addition to the Sponsor.

It would be particularly appropriate if one of the two Knights in attendance belonged to the Order of St. Gregory the Great, the other to the Order of Pope St. Sylvester.

Papal Knights can be assigned to other Bishops or high Prelates present, and others be given ceremonial tasks, liturgical tasks during Holy Mass or tasks assisting the Master of Ceremonies in other ways. It simply depends on how many uniformed Papal Knights are able to attend.

Once the procession reaches the altar, the Papal Knights will take their allocated positions. Those who will read the Lesson or bring the offerings to the Celebrant, should be assigned seats and kneelers in the most practical location.

The Sponsor should take his place near the Bishop who will perform the investiture, and a seat and kneeler should be provided for him.

Seating arrangements for Knights in attendance on other dignitaries must also be provided, and the Knights should be able to study a plan of these arrangements before they enter the Cathedral. It would be appropriate to have such a plan displayed in the room where the Knights robe.

The Master of Ceremonies will decide with the Bishop at what moment during the Mass the investiture will take place, and at the arranged time, the Bishop will ask the officiating Knight or the Chaplain to the Papal Knights to bring the candidates for investiture before him.

The Right Reverend Mgr. James Hannigan, Bishop of Menevia and Chairman of the Education Council of the Bishops Conference of England and Wales, celebrated the capitular Mass in Westminster Cathedral for the investiture of Mr. Terence Casey, C.B.E., as a Knight of the Pontifical Equestrian Order of St. Gregory the Great.

2.

THE INVESTITURE

The investiture from now on is the same as that described in Chapter V: *INVESTITURE BY THE LOCAL BISHOP IN THE PARISH CHURCH.*

At the end of the Mass, the Master of Ceremonies will make arrangements for a verger to lead the robed Knights and Dames of other Orders from their places to the sacristy or to the room set aside for them. This procesion is immediately followed by the Bishop's procession in the same order as it entered the Cathedral.

When the Bishop who conducted the investiture reaches the front row where the newly invested Knights and recipients of Papal Awards are seated, they will be invited by the Master of Ceremonies to join the procession, walking in the following order in front of the Bishop: recipients of the Award *Benemerenti* and *Pro Ecclesia et Pontifice*, Knights, Knights

After the Gospel, the Master of Ceremonies of the Cathedral, Fr. Daniel Cronin, led the Bishop to a throne which had been placed in front of the altar.

Bishop Hannigan asked the Chaplain to the Papal Knights in Great Britain, Fr. V. Felzman, D.D., who acted as the Candidate's Sponsor, to bring Mr. Terence Casey to the altar for the investiture.

The Bishop invested the Candidate with the insignia of a Knight of the Pontifical Equestrian Order of St. Gregory the Great.

(Left) The newly invested Knight returned to his place after the ceremony. (Right) Bishop Hannigan pays tribute to Chevalier Terence Casey, CBE, KSG, for his outstanding services to Catholic education.

After the final Blessing, the Bishop left the Cathedral in solemn procession. The new Knight, his family and friends were led by the Chaplain to the Papal Knights to the Library of Archbishop's House for a reception. Sadly, Chevalier Terence Casey died three weeks after being invested a Knight of the Pontifical Equestrian Order of St. Gregory the Great.

Commander and Knights Grand Cross of the Order of Pope St. Sylvester, Knights, Knights Commander and Knights Grand Cross of the Order of St. Gregory of the Great.

As the Order of Pius IX is only conferred in the Vatican, no particular provision has been made so far, but Pian Knights would follow the Knights of St. Gregory the Great.

If a Knight on whom the Pian Order has been conferred were to ask his Local Bishop for an investiture during Holy Mass, it would take the same form as that for the other Pontifical Orders of Knighthood, substituting "The Order of Pius IX" for the names of the other Orders. The text, when describing the Order to the new Pian Knight and the Congregation is:

> "The Order of Pius IX was founded in 1847 by Pope Pius IX to reward conspicuous deeds of merit in Church and Society. Also known as the Pian Order, it is today conferred mainly on diplomats accredited to the Holy See, visiting statesmen or for personal services rendered to the Holy Father".

3.

GUIDELINES CONCERNING PRECEDENCE

The question of precedence among Orders of Knighthood is only being dealt with in the context of an investiture of Papal Knights in a Cathedral, though the same criteria should apply to tall religious ceremonies unless the services are organised by other chivalric Orders, when the Papal Knights take the place allocated to them by their hosts.

Pontifical Equestrian Orders should never be drawn into disputes on precedence, and Masters of Ceremonies should always bear this in mind. In the context of religious services, Papal Knights are not subject to the same chivalric rules of precedence as other Orders.

As much as Pope St. Pius X decreed that Papal Knights have their place in the papal *cortège*, so they have their place in the *cortèges* of cardinals, archbishops and bishops, and not in religious processions in front, between or behind other Orders of Knighthood.

Concerning the Pontifical Orders of Knighthood, Pope St. Pius X said: "There is a fundamental difference between the Pontifical Orders of Knighthood and the Religious-Military, but not Pontifical, Orders of Knighthood, such as the Sovereign Military Order of Malta and the Equestrian Order of the Holy Sepulchre of Jerusalem. Their foundation was the result of private initiative, later approved by the Papacy, but from their very beginning, like the other early Monastic-Military Orders of Knighthood, they were naturally oriented towards the Church by reason of their constitution and motivation. The aforesaid Orders are fully recognised by the Holy See in their respective different status".

Pope St. Pius X spoke as Sovereign and Grand Master of the Pontifical Orders of Knighthood, and although no Pontiff exercised the *de facto* powers of a sovereign ruler over territory between 1870 and 1929, his rights as Sovereign and Grand Master of the Pontifical Orders of Knighthood have always remained inviolable in International Law. Pontifical Orders of Knighthood were founded by Supreme Pontiffs and they have an order of precedence among themselves which has been determined by the Holy See.

Judging on these facts, a Master of Ceremonies can, if he so wishes, apply the international rules of precedence according to the date of foundation to other Orders taking part in the religious service. For example, the years of foundation recognised by the Holy See are 1070 for the Sovereign Military Order of Malta and 1099 for the Equestrian Order of the Holy Sepulchre of Jerusalem.

The following order of precedence for the Pontifical Orders of Knighthood applies:

1) The Supreme Order of Christ;
2) The Order of the Golden Spur;
3) The Order of Pius IX;
4) The Order of St. Gregory the Great;
5) The Order of Pope St. Sylvester.

The number of Pontifical Orders of Knighthood is given as five because the Golden Collar of the Pian Order is an extension to the Order of Pius IX. However, the Orders of Christ and of the Golden Spur and the Golden Collar of the Pian Order are conferred on Heads of State only.

4.

INVESTITURE OF A PAPAL KNIGHT IN A CATHEDRAL HALL OR IN THE THRONE ROOM

Attending investitures in the Cathedral Hall or the Throne Room is usually by invitation only, although the invitation will include attending the Eucharist which may be celebrated before the investiture.

The Administrator of the Cathedral should be informed well in advance which guests of honour will attend the investiture and also if any of the invited guests need to have special facilities provided. He prepares a list of the guests of honour so that they can be welcomed personally by the Bishop.

The Bishop may delegate the task of opening the formal procedure to the Administrator or another dignitary of the Cathedral.

When the guests are assembled, the Hon. Secretary of the Papal Knights or a senior Knight will lead his uniformed confrères into the hall, followed by the Bishop's entourage. The Sponsor will walk in front of the Bishop who will conduct the investiture, and two Knights in attendance will bring the procession to a close.

The senior Papal Knight will guide his uniformed confrères to their allocated places and the Master of Ceremonies will guide the Bishop's entourage to a pre-arranged place. If the Master of Ceremonies does not take part in the function outside the Cathedral, the senior Knight will also guide the Bishop's entourage to the pre-arranged place. The Sponsor will take up his position near the Bishop and will hand him the insignia for conferment at the investiture.

The candidates for investiture will have been placed in front, facing the Bishop, and they will step forward when the Bishop asks them to do so. The investiture is a solemn function; drinks and refreshments should be offered only after the formal ceremony has been concluded.

The procedure is opened with the welcome of the guests and continues as in Chapter V: *INVESTITURE OF A PAPAL KNIGHT IN THE PARISH HALL.* If there are several candidates for investiture, the Sponsor will inform the Bishop of the order in which candidates should be called to come forward.

The Bishop begins the ceremony with the section:

"The Pontifical Order of St. Gregory the Great [or: . . . of Pope St. Sylvester; or both Orders]was founded . . . etc.", followed by the texts dealing with the Papal Awards *Pro Ecclesia et Pontifice* and *Benemerenti* if applicable.

After the Bishop has completed an investiture or a conferment of an Award, the Knight or the recipient of the Award will bow to the Bishop and return to the body of the hall, and the next candidate will be called to come forward. After the last investiture or conferment, the Bishop may address the guests, after which he announces that the formal function has ended and refreshments will now be served.

WESTMINSTER CATHEDRAL

PAPAL KNIGHTS IN GREAT BRITAIN
ORDERS OF PIUS IX, ST. GREGORY AND ST. SYLVESTER

CELEBRATION OF THE EUCHARIST

ON THE OCCASION OF

SIR HAROLD HOOD, Bt.

BEING CREATED

KNIGHT GRAND CROSS
OF THE ORDER OF ST. GREGORY THE GREAT

PRINCIPAL CELEBRANT
FR. VLADIMIR FELZMANN
CHAPLAIN TO THE PAPAL KNIGHTS IN GREAT BRITAIN

THURSDAY, 5th FEBRUARY, 1987
6.00 p.m.

CHAPTER SEVEN

PROMOTION WITHIN A PONTIFICAL EQUESTRIAN ORDER

As stated earlier, when a Papal Knight is promoted within his Order or receives Papal Knighthood in another Order, there is no need for a second investiture. It is most likely that he will receive the new insignia at the Bishop's residence. However, this does not imply that such an occasion should not be celebrated with a Eucharist.

In 1987, His Holiness Pope John Paul II created Sir Harold Hood, Bt., KCSG, a Knight Grand Cross of the Pontifical Equestrian Order of St. Gregory the Great on the occasion of Sir Harold's retirement after twenty years as Chairman of the Association of Papal Knights in Great Britain.

His Eminence the Cardinal Archbishop of Westminster invited the family and friends of Sir Harold to a celebration of the Eucharist, followed by the conferment of the honour and a reception in the Throne Room at Archbishop's House. The Liturgy of St. Gregory the Great was

The Cardinal Archbishop of Westminster

requests the pleasure of the company of

at a Reception
following the celebration of Mass of St. Gregory the Great,
in Westminster Cathedral Hall, Ambrosden Avenue, SW1, at 6.00pm
on Thursday, 5th February, 1987.

After the Mass, Sir Harold Hood, Bt, will be presented with
the Insignia of Knight Grand Cross of the Papal Order of
St. Gregory the Great.

R.S.V.P. on enclosed card
The Private Secretary,
Archbishop's House,
Westminster, SW1P 1QJ.

Please present this card.

The invitation of His Eminence the Cardinal Archbishop of Westminster.

His Eminence Basil Cardinal Hume, OSB, Archbishop of Westminster, confers the insignia of a Knight Grand Cross of the Pontifical Equestrian Order of St. Gregory the Great on Sir Harold Hood, Bt., who was already wearing the silver-embroidered uniform of his new rank. Lady Hood (right) was the first to congratulate Sir Harold.

concelebrated by eight priests in Westminster Cathedral Hall; the Principal Celebrant was the Chaplain to the Papal Knights, Fr. Vladimir Felzmann. Many Knights attended in uniform.

Sir Harold Hood, Bt., already wearing the uniform of a Knight Grand Cross, gave the Reading, *Isaiah 61: 1–3*, and the Hon. Secretary to the Papal Knights, Brigadier Gordon Viner, KSG, gave the Bidding Prayers. A very moving moment was the *Sign of Peace*, when the folk choir which had earlier led the congregation in the Peruvian *Gloria* did so now with the *Shalom, my friend, shalom, shalom*. It was a year ago that in the same hall Sir Sigmund Sternberg, a Jew, had been invested by His Eminence Basil Cardinal Hume, OSB, as a Knight Commander of the Order of St. Gregory the Great.

After the celebration of the Eucharist, Sir Harold Hood, Bt., GCSG, his family and friends witnessed in the Throne Room of Archbishop's House Cardinal Hume conferring upon Sir Harold the insignia of a Knight Grand Cross.

INDUCTION AND INVESTITURE
OF

SIR SIGMUND STERNBERG

as
KNIGHT COMMANDER
OF THE PONTIFICAL EQUESTRIAN ORDER
OF ST. GREGORY THE GREAT

BY
HIS EMINENCE
BASIL CARDINAL HUME, O.S.B.
ARCHBISHOP OF WESTMINSTER

at 5.30 p.m. on TUESDAY, 4 MARCH, 1986

in WESTMINSTER CATHEDRAL HALL,
AMBROSEDEN AVENUE, LONDON, SW1

CHAPTER EIGHT

WHICH PAPAL ORDER CAN BE BESTOWED ON A NON-CATHOLIC, AND CAN A NON-CATHOLIC PAPAL KNIGHT BE INVESTED?

Before continuing with matters of etiquette and procedure it is necessary that these questions are answered first because they have been asked many times since more non-Catholics are now being honoured by the Supreme Pontiff with a Knighthood.

Non-Catholic Heads of State can receive the Order of the Golden Spur if they are Christians but not necessarily Roman Catholics, and the Golden Collar of the Pian Order if they are non-Christians.

The Orders of Pius IX and of Pope St. Sylvester have been conferred on non-Catholics and non-Christians for many years.

The questions I endeavour to answer here have been put to me many times. They have been prompted by a specific precedent which was set on 4 March 1986 when Sir Sigmund Sternberg, a prominent Jew who is active in Christian-Jewish relations and particularly in Catholic-Jewish relations, was created a Knight Commander of the Equestrian Pontifical Order of St. Gregory the Great. I was asked to devise a special rite of investiture under the spiritual guidance of Right Reverend Mgr. Gerald Mahon, Bishop in West London and a member of the Executive of the Council for Christians and Jews.

Because we are dealing here with important precedents which serve as guidelines for the future, it is necessary to be clear and unambiguous, both when asking the questions and when giving the answers. It is easy to sweep delicate matters or subjects which might cause embarrassment under the proverbial carpet. To do this here would serve nobody and only cause confusion in the future. I therefore repeat the questions exactly as they were put to me, and I endeavour to answer them. I shall also quote His Eminence Basil Cardinal Hume, O.S.B., Archbishop of Westminster, who had been asked by His Holiness Pope John Paul II to conduct the investiture of Sir Sigmund Sternberg in his name and on his behalf.

I would give the wrong impression if I were to suggest that the first question was only being asked in England. It was even more often asked in Rome because some people held strong views on the subject. They spoke to me quite frankly, but without any ethnic prejudice, about a matter which they considered could weaken fundamental principles of Roman Catholicism. The questions were specific and referred to the Pontifical Equestrian Order of St. Gregory the Great only. Without exception those who asked it added that they felt the Order of Pope St. Sylvester would have been a more appropriate Honour to have bestowed on a non-Christian:

1) "Can the Pontifical Equestrian Order of St. Gregory the Great be conferred upon a non-Catholic and even on a non-Christian, for example a Jew, considering the criteria laid down for being honoured with an appointment to this Order?"

2) "Can a non-Catholic and especially a non-Christian be invested, bearing in mind the commitment a Catholic Knight is expected to make during his investiture?"

The *CODEX IURIS CANONICI* does not give any guidance as to the conferment of Papal Honours, but those who attribute an almost sacramental character to a Papal Knighthood must change their views. It would, however, be advisable not to conduct the investiture of a non-Catholic Papal Knight during a celebration of the Eucharist.

The occasional criticism levelled at me for having devised a ceremony of investiture, the prime objective of which appeared to have been to make concessions, is not only quite unfounded but illogical. There has never been a procedure of investiture before which could have served as a guideline or precedent to which I could adhere.

This first investiture was devised with the unstinting help of Bishop Mahon and Fr. V. Felzmann, Chaplain to the Papal Knights in Great Britain. Investitures for Catholic Papal Knights were devised later because of the requests of Papal Knights who felt that some standard precedure for an investiture was desirable. Bishop Mahon, who whole-heartedly supported such an idea, Fr. Vladimir Felzmann, Fr. Adrian Arrowsmith and others worked very hard and they paid attention to minute details. Their wish was to ensure that the rite of an investiture for Catholic Papal Knights would be an integral part of the Eucharist during which it would take place, and that such an investiture would not lose its liturgical significance if the candidate were to be invested after celebrating the Eucharist, for example in a Parish Hall.

Because no precedent existed for investitures, the second question is directly concerned with one paragraph in the ceremony which was later introduced as an essential part of the procedure for a Catholic candidate. This paragraph was, however, not included in the investiture ceremony for Sir Sigmund Sternberg. It concerns the fidelity to God, the Supreme Pontiff, the Holy See and the Church, which the Catholic Knight promises the Bishop who invests him.

The first question had been answered, even before anyone thought of asking it, by a dedication the late Archbishop H. E. Cardinale wrote in 1982: *"Pontifex Maximus qui in Universa Ecclesia Catholica sub Deo omnium Fons est Honorum"* — The Supreme Pontiff is under God the Source of all Honours in the Universal Catholic Church.

I would add that the Supreme Pontiff is *fons et origo* — fount and origin — of all Honours; all Pontifical Equestrian Orders are in the gift of the Supreme Pontiff, and they have been instituted, extended and revised by successive Popes.

There is no Pontifical Decree or Papal Brief which places any restrictions on a Supreme Pontiff with regard to the awarding of Pontifical Knighthoods. The Papal Letter of Paul VI, reserving the Supreme Order of Christ for Roman Catholics, and opening the Order of the Golden Spur to Christians as well as the Golden Collar of the Pian Order to non-Christians, was a guideline for the remaining years of his pontificate, but no Pontiff can lay down irrevocable rules for his successor. If, for example, a reigning Pope wishes to change the procedure of awarding the three highest Honours, he can do so.

However, no Pope has ever given a ruling which could be cited as a precedent for the conferments of the ranks of Knight, Knight Commander or Knight Grand Cross in the Pontifical Equestrian Orders of Pius IX, Gregory the Great and Pope St. Sylvester. This century has seen many changes in the attitude of the Supreme Pontiffs and in the guidance they have given to the Church with regard to inter-denominational and inter-faiths relations. Successive Popes have removed many barriers between Catholics and non-Catholics, and they have built bridges across gulfs which both sides could use in their approach towards each other. Of particular significance have been the declarations of successive Popes concerning Judaism.

Since Pope John XXIII first welcomed Archbishop Dr. Fisher of Canterbury, all successive Pontiffs have welcomed the leaders of other Christian denominations as their Brothers in Christ.

Never in the history of the Holy Roman Church had a Supreme Pontiff set foot in a Synagogue until Pope John Paul II did so in Rome in 1986.

Nobody thinks of Pope Pius XII as a Pontiff who would have sacrificed one principle of Catholic truth, or showed weakness in upholding Catholic values and especially the pre-eminent position of the Vicar of Christ. Although some have tried to portray Pius XII as intolerant and uncaring for those who did not embrace the Catholic Faith, the true facts are well known. Pius XII spoke out on behalf of his persecuted Jewish brothers and sisters, he opened the doors of the Vatican to them and gave thousands of them shelter, placing them under his personal protection. Pope John XXIII, when working as Nuncio during the war, made it his special mission to save as many Jews from the evils of their persecutors as was humanily possible. His successor, Paul VI, worked at the highest level of diplomacy in the Vatican during the pontificate of Pius XII. Mons. Giovanni Battista Montini was instrumental in carrying out the will of Pope Pius XII in saving the lives of many Jews in Rome.

I believe the reason that these questions have been asked at all, is the different values which are attributed to Pontifical Knighthoods. It is well known that the Pontifical Equestrian Order of St. Gregory the Great is awarded to gentlemen for their past loyalty and outstanding service to the Holy See and the Church and that unswerving loyalty is expected of them in the future. I know of no British Papal Knight of St. Gregory whose loyalty and devotion to his Sovereign and country have been in any way placed in jeopardy by his loyalty to God, the Holy Father, the Holy See and the Church. On the contrary, His Eminence Agostino Cardinal Casaroli, the Secretary of State, who has been endowed with the powers and duties formerly exercised by the Grand Chancellor of the Pontifical Equestrian Orders, has defined what this loyalty implies: any Papal Knight practicing that unswerving loyalty in his daily life bears witness at the same time to his deep loyalty to his Sovereign and love for his country. He has been honoured, and the honour was well deserved, but it committed him to "fighting evil, promoting good and defending the weak and oppressed against injustice".

The second question, as to whether a non-Christian, a Jew, could be invested can also be answered in the affirmative. Rather then presenting a justification for the decision to 'induct and invest' Sir Sigmund Sternberg into the Pontifical Equestrian Order of St. Gregory the Great, I reiterate the criteria upon which that decision was taken by His Holiness Pope John Paul II and carried out by His Eminence Basil Cardinal Hume, OSB, Archbishop of Westminster. His Eminence, speaking on behalf of the Supreme Pontiff and for himself, presented not only the most convincing proof of Sir Sigmund Sternberg's merits and for deserving the honour of a Knight Commander of the Order of St. Gregory the Great, but the reasons for investing him with this high honour.

His Eminence, having invested the candidate, on behalf of His Holiness Pope John Paul II who had expressly asked him to carry out this duty, addressed the Papal Knights and the many guests present:

"In creating Sir Sigmund Sternberg a Knight Commander of the Order of St. Gregory the Great, the Catholic Church is bestowing on him a public sign of its respect, recognition and appreciation. And since the knighthood is conferred for the distinguished contribution Sir Sigmund has made at home and abroad to Christian-Jewish relations, this must be seen also as a gesture of sincere friendship on the part of the Catholic Church to the whole Jewish people.

"I want, in particular, to speak about the relationship that must obtain between Catholics and the Jewish people. Increasingly in our day, and belatedly, Catholics like other Christians acknowledge the debt of gratitude they owe to the Jewish people and recognise the Jewish origins of the Christian Church. We have become more profoundly conscious of the Jewish soil that nourished our Christian roots. One cannot begin to understand Jesus Christ and the significance of his life and teaching without knowledge of his people, their history and beliefs. He was a Jew and our religious heritage, like his, is that of the Law and the Prophets. The Christian Eucharist we celebrate owes its origin to the Passover meal; the daily prayers we offer, particularly the Divine Office sung in our monasteries, convents and cathedrals, is created out of the Psalms of David. The Chosen People have taught Christians how to pray; they have pioneered the paths of God's revelation; they have enriched us with basic moral concepts and precious principles about the dignity of man, about human rights, liberty and justice. The Covenant between God and His People once made cannot be broken; it stands unrevoked. It is that which commands our reverence and our affection.

"Christians, then should regard the Jewish people and its faith with respect, gratitude and understanding. We condemn anti-Semitism in any form; we repudiate all discrimination, suspicion and prejudice. Mindful of the long history of Christian intolerance and persecution, we can only dissociate ourselves wholeheartedly from past injustice and attempt, however inadequately, to make amends for the crimes committed against the Jewish people.

"I cannot personally think about the Shoa — the Holocaust — without a feeling of total revulsion and deep sadness. The pictures that have recorded that chapter in the history of the world remain indelibly impressed on all our minds. The Shoa is one of the most shameful episodes in our human story.

"Part of our atonement must be the sustained attempt to study the richness of Jewish thought and religious genius throughout the ages. The confrontation and incomprehension of the past must give way to the dialogue and understanding of today. We condemn and reject all ill-conceived and insensitive attempts — sometimes imported from abroad — to subject Jews, especially the young and vulnerable, to aggressive and systematic indoctrination.

"I am sure that our Jewish friends understand that any relationship of trust and respect has to be a growing-together in mutual knowledge and sympathy. We hope that you will continue to explore our tradition and our beliefs and to respect our convictions as we do yours.

"The Second Vatican Council, some twenty years ago, represented for Catholics a new and contemporary effort to interpret for our generation the message of Jesus Christ. Its Declaration on the Relation of the Church to Non-Christian Religions (known by the Latin words *Nostra Ætate*) was of immense significance. It lays down guiding principles for dialogue with the world's great faiths and, in particular, with the faith of the Jewish people. It acknowledges explicitly the unique bond between Christianity and Judaism and calls for mutual knowledge and esteem. The Council declared: 'The Catholic Church has a sincere respect for those ways of acting and living, those moral and doctrinal teachings which may differ in many respects from what she holds and teaches, but which none-the-less often reflect the brightness of that Truth which is the light of all men'. But the Council went on in the same passage to emphasise that the Catholic Church — and now I quote — '. . . proclaims, and is bound to proclaim unceasingly, Christ, who is the way, the truth and the life' (John 14:6). In him men find the fulness of their religious life and in him God has reconciled all things to himself (cf. 2 Cor. 5:18–19).

"She, therefore, urges Catholics, using prudence and charity, to join members of other religions in discussions and collaboration. While bearing witness to their own Christian faith and life, they must acknowledge those good spiritual and moral elements and social and cultural values found in other religions, and preserve and encourage them (*Nostra Ætate* 2).

"So this, then, is the true respect and honesty that ought to be found in our relationship to each other. There must be fidelity to our faiths, frank and yet gentle witness to the truth within us, care to foster and preserve what is good and true in others. We must be aware of each other, welcoming each other, be accessible to each other, being ready and eager at all times to give an account to anyone of the faith which is in us. This is not religious aggression; it is a ministry, a service, to the truth.

"Christian Jewish relations will continue to develop if on both sides we commit ourselves to that practice of prayer, which is the very soul of religious dialogue. It is, surely, entirely right to recognise what we are, as human beings, most authentically what we are supposed to be, when preoccupied with seeking those glimpses of the glory of God as it is reflected in His Creation and expressed through His Word. From this comes our worship and praise. This we can share together.

"So we shall continue to approach each other in a spirit of genuine concern and love. Dialogue in the pursuit of truth must at all times be an expression of love and mutual trust.

"I believe that this is the path marked out for us. In this spirit there can be no ambiguity in a Jewish believer accepting a Catholic honour — only the affirmation of shared roots and a common bond."

Basil Cardinal Hume, O.S.B.
Archbishop of Westminster
has pleasure in inviting

to the Induction and Investiture of

Sir Sigmund Sternberg, Kt.,

as a Knight Commander of the Pontifical Equestrian Order of St Gregory the Great
at Westminster Cathedral Hall, Ambroseden Avenue London S.W.1,
on Tuesday, 4 March 1986 at 5.30 pm
followed by a Reception in the Throne Room of Archbishops' House

Dress:
Formal canonical
Papal Knights in uniforms & decorations
Knights & Dames E.O.H.S.
Morning Dress
Dark lounge suit/Day dress

(ON ACCEPTANCE A PROGRAMME WILL BE SENT TO YOU)

R.S.V.P.
to the Secretary
Archbishop's House
Ambroseden Avenue
London SW1 by not later
than Tuesday 25 Feb.

The invitation of His Eminence the Cardinal Archbishop of Westminster.

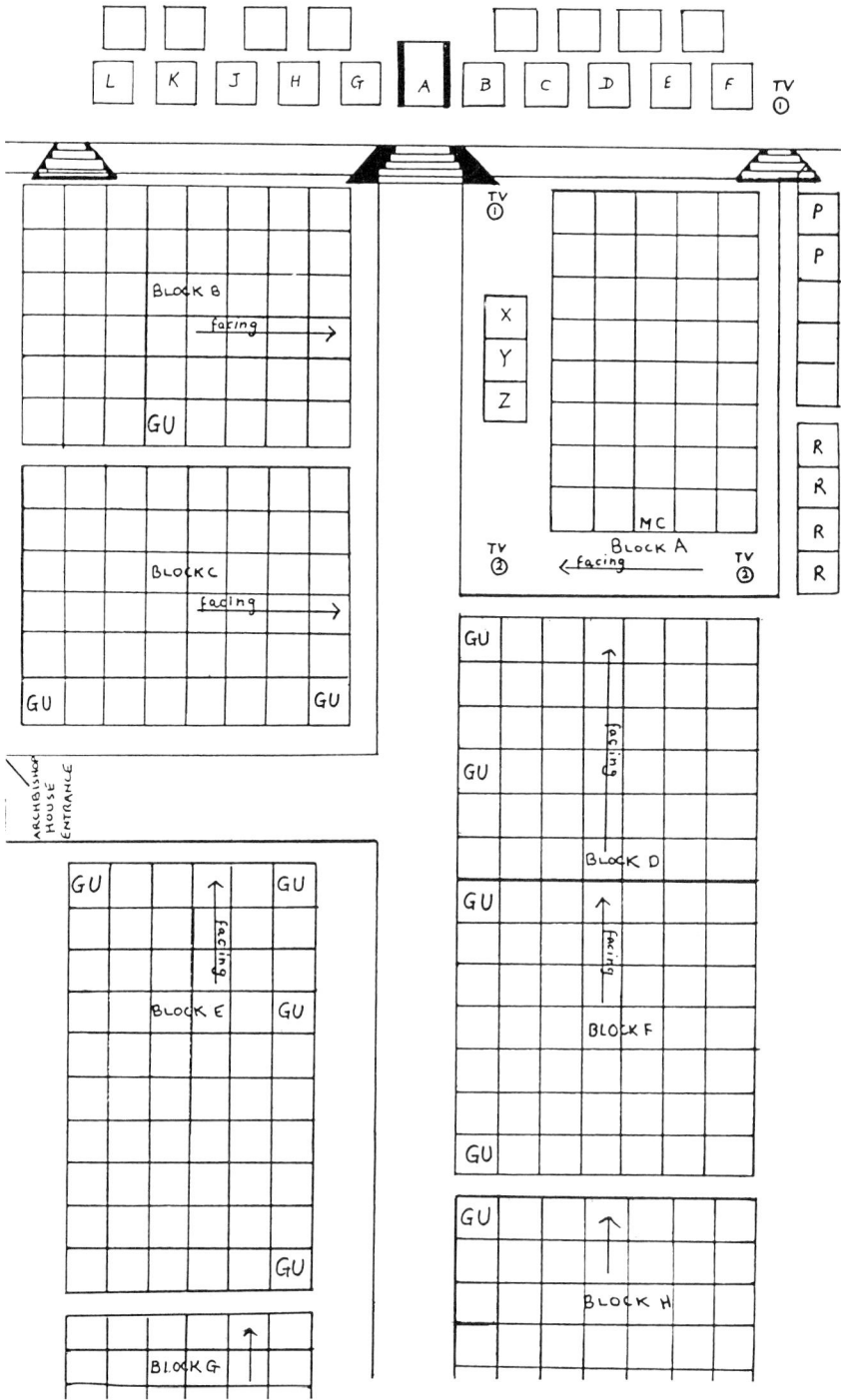

Plan of Westminster Cathedral Hall for the investiture. Block A faced Blocks B & C; All other Blocks face towards the stage. XYZ were the seats for the Candidate and his Sponsors; GU were Gentlemen Ushers and TV the television cameras.

CHAPTER NINE

A PRECEDENT FOR AN INVESTITURE
OF A NON-CATHOLIC PAPAL KNIGHT

Early in 1986, I was asked to devise the investiture for Sir Sigmund Sternberg. This was, to the best of my knowledge, the first investiture of a Papal Knight since 1905.

With regard to the particular procedure, I refer once more to the literal meaning of the word 'investiture'. The candidate to be invested had acquired the uniform of a Knight Commander of the Order of St. Gregory the Great before the procedure took place. A Cardinal, representing His Holiness Pope John Paul II, by conferring the Cross on the newly appointed Papal Knight completed the insignia (which comprise the uniform and the decoration). The Papal Knight was therefore robed with the garment, decorated with the Cross, and endowed with the rank and office of a Knight Commander of the Order of St. Gregory the Great.

The circumstances surrounding the event were also unusual. A spiritual dimension was added by the presence of eminent Church leaders, such as a retired Archbishop of Canterbury, leaders of other Christian Churches, the Chief Rabbi of the Commonwealth, several Rabbis from Britain and abroad, Archbishops and Bishops of the Roman Catholic Church and the Chargé d'Affaires of the Apostolic Nunciature in Great Britain representing the Holy See.

The event was timed to take place shortly before Pope John Paul II's visit to the Synagogue in Rome on 13 April 1986, and the newly invested Papal Knight Commander had been asked to attend this historic occasion in Rome, wearing his uniform of a Papal Knight Commander of St. Gregory the Great and exercising his duty and prerogative as a Papal Knight of attending upon the Supreme Pontiff.

Leading representatives of public life also came to the investiture, among them the Lord High Chancellor of the Realm, the Speaker of the House of Commons, the Earl Marshal of England, Members of the Government and of other political parties, both in the House of Lords and the House of Commons; representing several countries, many Ambassadors accredited to the Court of St. James also attended. The Cardinal Archbishop of Westminster conducted the investiture, and Mgr. Gerald Mahon, Bishop in West London and a member of the Executive of the Council for Christians and Jews, was in over-all charge of the arrangements.

I had been asked to devise a short and dignified ceremony of investiture, and a procedure had to be worked out that would do justice to the concept of the inter-faith relations between Catholics and Jews.

With the help of Bishop Mahon, Brigadier Viner, KSG, and others I had to prepare two quite separate functions: a procedure for the investiture of a non-Catholic Knight and a major social function which would have the investiture as its highpoint.

It is unlikely that events like this will take place very often. However, if and when another non-Catholic Knight is to be invested, the guidelines now exist.

In this case, however, there were other complications not usually associated with the investiture of Papal Knights. As many of the guests were under the constant protection of the Special Branch or the Metropolitan Police Security Services, a team of trusted workers was needed to deal with the invitations and certain security matters and from whose number could be drawn the many Gentlemen Ushers needed in the Hall prior to the ceremony.

Brigadier G. Viner, a Knight of the Pontifical Equestrian Order of St. Gregory the Great and Honorary Secretary of the Association of Papal Knights in Great Britain, had taken on the responsibility for providing a special room and changing facilities for the many Papal Knights who attended in uniform, and together with his confrère Mr. A. M. A. Sczaniecki, a Knight Commander of the Pontifical Equestrian Order of Pope St. Sylvester, he also acted as one of Sir Sigmund Sternberg's sponsors.

The Chaplain to the Papal Knights, Fr. Felzmann, sub-Administrator of Westminster Cathedral, arranged for other Catholic Orders to send delegations. The Knights were in morning dress and the Dames in dark day dress, all with full decorations.

The seating arrangement was made partly to assist the television and press cameramen, partly to enable the guests to get a clear view of the stage where the Cardinal and the Guests of Honour were seated and the investiture took place. The arrangement also gave the guests a good view of the uniformed Papal Knights and prominent public figures.

The Hall was divided into blocks, those nearest to the stage facing each other; the Papal Knights in Block A, with the Ambassadors and public figures in Blocks B and C (see diagram of the Hall). Because considerably more guests had accepted the invitation than were expected to do so, two upper galleries had to be opened as well.

Twelve Gentlemen Ushers took up their positions in the Hall and checked that all arrangements had been made according to plan; two Ushers were on the stage, ready to lead the Guests of Honour to their seats and also to make any last-minute adjustment to the seating. In the event, the opening of the main doors for the guests was slightly delayed because the Metropolitan Police undertook a thorough search of the Hall, the galleries and the Throne Room with trained sniffer dogs.

The Master of Ceremonies met the Lord High Chancellor and the Speaker of the House of Commons when they arrived and took them to the Cardinal. He then informed His Eminence and the Guests of Honour of the order of the procession into the Hall, and their position in it.

It is obvious that this ceremony bears little resemblance to the usual investiture of a Papal Knight, but the special circumstances made these exceptional arrangements necessary.

The guests were requested to be in their seats early as the doors had to be closed at 5.20 p.m. The preliminary procedure was arranged as follows: delegations of Knights and Dames of other Catholic Orders entered the hall from Archbishop's House and took their seats at 5.15 p.m. Knights in uniform of the Pontifical Equestrian Orders, followed by the candidate for investiture and his two sponsors, entered the Hall in procession and took their seats at 5.25 p.m. At 5.30 p.m. the Cardinal's procession was met at the door leading from Archbishop's House by the Master of Ceremonies who led them to the steps to the stage; there the Gentlemen Ushers took each guest to the allocated place. The last person to ascend the steps to the stage was His Eminence Cardinal Hume who was seated in the centre.

At this point Bishop Mahon took charge of the procedure. Four microphones had been strategically placed on the stage so that no speaker had to wait for a microphone to be brought to him.

THE INVESTITURE

The procedure of investiture which follows can be easily modified and adapted to different requirements. It is possible that the ceremony as given in Chapter Five is more suitable to the occasion; the setting is less formal. The main objective of an investiture is to add a spiritual dimension to the conferment of a papal knighthood; there is no doubt that this was the case when Sir Sigmund Sternberg was invested. Although he was not asked to make a verbal commitment of loyalty to the Supreme Pontiff and the Holy See, his is a case where actions speak louder than words. Also, by acquiring the uniform of a Papal Knight, he had made a very clear commitment: he would fully participate in the activities of the Papal Knights and he attended upon the Supreme Pontiff not as a prominent member of the international

After the guests of honour took their places on the stage, His Eminence Basil Cardinal Hume, OSB, Archbishop of Westminster asked that the candidate, Sir Sigmund Sternberg, be brought forward. Among the guests of honour were the Lord High Chancellor, the Speaker of the House of Commons, the Chargé d'Affaires of the Apostolic Nunciature and the Chief Rabbi.

His Eminence Basil Cardinal Hume conferred the Cross of a Knight Commander on Sir Sigmund Sternberg. Brigadier C. G. T. Viner, CBE, MC, KSG, Hon. Secretary to the Papal Knights in Great Britain, assisted the Cardinal.

Brigadier Viner, a Knight of the Order of St. Gregory the Great, (left), and Mr. A. M. A. Sczaniecki, Knight Commander of the Order of Pope St. Sylvester, (right), were Sir Sigmund's Sponsors. After the investiture, Brigadier Viner asked permission of His Eminence to withdraw and lead the newly invested Knight Commander to his confrères, the Papal Knights.

The new Knight Commander (centre), and his Sponsors have taken their places in front of the Papal Knights. Facing the Knights on the other side of the aisle are ambassadors and members of both Houses of Parliament.

His Holiness Pope John Paul II with Sir Sigmund Sternberg, Kt., KCSG, JP, OH, who was a Papal Knight in attendance on the Supreme Pontiff at the Synagogue in Rome.

Jewish community but as a Papal Knight when he joined His Holiness Pope John Paul II at the Synagogue in Rome on 13 April 1986.

As stated earlier, Bishop Mahon took charge of the procedure of investiture, and from there on I reproduce the ceremony from the brochure:

His Excellency Bishop. Mahon will welcome the guests and invite His Eminence to begin the procedure of the investiture.

His Eminence Basil Cardinal Hume, OSB, will ask Sir Sigmund Sternberg to be presented to him:

"Will the Knight to be invested with the insignia of a Knight Commander of St. Gregory the Great be brought forward."

Sir Sigmund Sternberg, Kt., will be led to His Eminence by two confrères, a Knight of the Order of St. Gregory the Great and a Knight of the Order of Pope St. Silvester.

Brigadier C. G. T. Viner, CBE, MC, TD, KSG, Honorary Secretary of the Papal Knights in Great Britain, will present the new Knight:

116

"Your Eminence,

I have the honour of presenting Sir Sigmund Sternberg to be invested with the Cross of a Knight Commander of the Order of St. Gregory the Great."

As soon as Sir Sigmund has ascended the steps and taken his position on the stage, His Excellency Bishop Mahon will invite His Eminence to sit; the candidate remains standing. Bishop Mahon will first read from the constitution the criteria for a papal knighthood being bestowed, and then the definition of the rôle of a Papal Knight, given by the Papal Secretary of State, Agostino Cardinal Casaroli. The Bishop will then read the English translation of the Papal Brief creating Sir Sigmund Sternberg a Knight Commander of the Pontifical Equestrian Order of St. Gregory the Great:

"Your Eminence, Commendatore Sir Sigmund, The Order of St. Gregory the Great, founded in 1831 by Pope Gregory XVI, is conferred for outstanding services to the Holy See on gentlemen of proved loyalty.

"His Eminence the Papal Secretary of State has defined the rôle of a Pontifical Knight thus: 'Becoming a Knight does not merely mean receiving a title of honour, even though it is well deserved, but fighting evil, promoting good and defending the weak and oppressed against injustice.'

"The Papal Brief creating Sir Sigmund Sternberg a Knight Commander of the Pontifical Order of St. Gregory the Great, reads as follows:

[The Bishop reads the Papal Brief which is already given in the English translation in Chapter Five.]

Bishop Mahon will now turn to the Cardinal and ask him to invest Sir Sigmund Sternberg. One of the Sponsors, Brigadier Viner, will ascend the steps and assist His Eminence with the investiture. Together with the newly invested Knight he will bow to His Eminence, step down to his previous position and with new Knight Commander between his Sponsors, the Honorary Secretary of the Papal Knights will ask the permission of His Eminence to with draw:

"Your Eminence, Sir Sigmund Sternberg having been duly invested, we humbly ask your permission to withdraw and lead Sir Sigmund to his confrères the Papal Knights."

His Eminence will indicate his consent and the Knights return to their places.

There will now be four speakers to address the guests:

His Eminence Basil Cardinal Hume, OSB, Archbishop of Westminster;

The Very Reverend Chief Rabbi Sir Immanuel Jakobovits, President of the Council of Christians and Jews; The Most Rev. and Rt. Hon. The Lord Coggan, Hon. President of the International Council of Christians and Jews; and The Rev. Dr. Isaac Levy, Hon. Secretary of the Council of Christians and Jews.

His Excellency Bishop Mahon will bring the ceremony to a close at 6.10 p.m.

The Papal Knights with Sir Sigmund Sternberg, who is accompanied by his sponsors at the investiture, will leave Westminster Cathedral Hall and go to Archbishop's House. They are followed by His Eminence and the Guests of Honour. The Master of Ceremonies will conclude the formal procession, and all guests who attended the investiture are invited to Archbishop's House where a reception is given in the Throne Room (6.30–7.45 p.m.).

When all guests have arrived in the Throne Room, Sir Sigmund Sternberg, K.C.S.G., will briefly speak to the dignitaries and guests.

PART II

The Chapters in PART II arise directly or indirectly from the publication of the revised edition of *Orders of Knighthood, Awards and the Holy See* (October 1985), and they deal mainly with the clarification or definition, and also the qualification of terms used in connection with Orders of Knighthood. It was impossible to anticipate the questions and, sometimes, problems arose after the subject matter had been presented. My main objective has been to qualify earlier statements.

Although lessons can be learned from the chapter on the *Bullarium Romanum* and the *Bullaria* themselves, had I not published a note I found among Archbishop Cardinale's papers, I would not have needed to research this subject. However, sooner or later the *Bullarium Romanum* would have entered the debate on Catholic Orders of Chivalry, especially on the part of defenders of privileges.

The questions as to whether Orders have been suppressed or abolished were mainly asked in the context of extinct Catholic Orders, which have been, and probably will continue to be, at the root of most disputes.

Endeavouring to understand the subtleties involved in placing an Order of Knighthood or an Award of Merit in abeyance meant entering a grey area of chivalry. The reader may well ask why I took unofficial counsel from a senior member of the Secretariat of State when discussing the procedure of placing an Order in abeyance; the reason is that only an appointed Pontifical Tribunal could recommend procedures which, if adopted, would express the view of the Holy See. On reflection, however, I do not believe the subject is important enough to justify the appointment of a Pontifical Commission to deliberate on it for a year or longer.

Last, but far from least, I felt compelled to return to the unsavoury subject of self-styled orders. Four years of having to deal with them have broadened my experience considerably. Self-styled orders, bogus titles, false diplomatic passports and a variety of dubious activities going on in the world — perhaps underworld is a better description — of pseudo-chivalry are, I sincerely believe, beyond the visible horizon of the Holy Father and most members of the Roman Curia. But all these distasteful activities have become very much a reality among masses of gullible and naive people who spend their hard-earned money on buying themselves some decoration or purported honour which is their Kingdom of Heaven on earth!

Of course, the Holy See condemns such practices and publishes the condemnations in *L'Osservatore Romano*, but how many read that very worthy and excellent newspaper? *L'Osservatore Romano* restricts itself to rather abstract condemnations. The last four years have taught me how these purveyors of orders, titles and "diplomatic" passports operate. I have seen mail-order catalogues offering 'honours' for sale using unlawfully but with impunity, the names of legitimate Orders of Knighthood, the names people of the highest integrity and even the name of the Pope himself to perpetrate their unscrupulous schemes. Experiencing the reality of what goes on in the name of the Holy Roman Church had a more sobering effect on me and many friends to whom I showed the evidence than statistics and warnings against this or that organisation. The ink has not dried on the copy of *L'Osservatore Romano* which carries such a warning, when those named have changed their names and carry on as before, claiming their *"ipso facto"* recognition by the Holy See.

The chapters in Part II contain much of what I wish I had known before I embarked on the task of revising *Orders of Knighthood, Awards and the Holy See*; but as in so many walks of life, personal experience is still the best teacher.

CHAPTER ONE

"SCATTERED AND HARD-TO-FIND SOURCES"

Even after the publication of the revised edition of *Orders of Knighthood, Awards and the Holy See* in October 1985, requests were still being received for the reassessment of the status of some Orders so that they could be placed among the extant Catholic Orders of Knighthood. Others wanted to see certain Dynastic Orders placed in abeyance, but by far the greatest number of letters came from the self-styled Orders which were listed in Chapter Eleven. In most cases, the requests, queries or complaints had arisen because of the publication of the first authoritative account of the Holy See's views on, and attitudes to, Orders of Knighthood.

Besides the correction of some minor points in the entries on some Orders, several serious and complex problems were raised. I sometimes believed I had taken charge of Pandora's Box of Chivalry when I had agreed to become the *Revisore* for Archbishop Cardinale's book, and that I had opened it when I began my work.

I shall return to the subject of the self-styled orders in the last chapter of Part II; it is a sad and pathetic subject, though looking at some of the astute and crafty purveyors of bogus orders, it is impossible to feel sorry for most of them.

However, I also received many reasonable requests and enquiries, and, as I indicated, some unforeseen, and complex, problems arose which urgently needed solving.

These problems were brought about firstly by Archbishop Cardinale's arbitrary use of the terms 'suppressed' and 'abolished' and his classification of all such Orders as 'extinct'. A matter which also caused much confusion was the incorrect or misleading information supplied by some governments when referring to Orders which had been conferred by former regimes or had belonged to Royal Houses of former Sovereigns before the political structure in their countries changed. This information was not given deliberately; I am sure that the informants believed sincerely that their definitions and statements reflected the correct status of the relevant Orders. As more and more facts came to light, one of the main causes for the misunderstanding was found in the difference of interpretation of events or facts and in the translation of words in two or more languages.

Besides the many chivalric Orders that were founded between the eleventh and thirteenth centuries, which sometimes did not even survive their founders, or, as in some cases, were only planned without ever having been properly instituted, and those, the history of which is shrouded in legend, there remains a substantial number of Orders of Knighthood which are a nightmare to their chroniclers: at one moment flourishing, then placed in abeyance, recalled from abeyance and reconstituted, then suppressed and revived again — most *ad infinitum*; some were amalgamated with another Order and some were abolished.

It has been suggested that more categories should have been created by Mgr. Cardinale to accommodate some of the dubious Orders to which one might give the benefit of doubt. I believe that the categories chosen by Archbishop Cardinale are quite sufficient, with one exception: the Teutonic Order had been placed in the Chapter dealing with Religious but not Pontifical Orders of Knighthood. The Order had lost its chivalric status in 1929 when it became a clerical Order and was placed under the jurisdiction of the Sacred Congregation for the Religious. It should therefore have been correctly placed among the 'Extinct Catholic Orders of Knighthood'. However, because the present Catholic Order in Austria has retained many traditions from its past, I felt justified in adding a special category to the revised edition: 'A transformed religious Order of Knighthood'.

As far as Chapter Nine is concerned ('Extinct Catholic Orders of Knighthood'), four types of Orders belong there: those that did not survive their founder, legendary orders, those which are only mentioned in some ancient chronicle but lacking any other evidence of their existence, and those which have been lawfully abolished. The abolition of a Catholic Order of Knighthood is not as simple as many believe it to be; however, once an Order has been properly abolished, nothing can revive it. The process of abolishing a Catholic Order of Knighthood is, in fact, so complex in International Law, that I felt it necessary to give it a special section.

There is genuine confusion about the legal meaning of he terms 'abolished' and 'suppressed'. When I mentioned the arbitrary use of the two terms by Archbishop Cardinale, I did not wish to imply criticism, or impute carelessness. When he embarked on the project of writing the first ever authoritative work on Catholic Orders of Knighthood, nobody could have foreseen the complications and hidden pitfalls, sometimes political problems, which made it necessary in the end to obtain the views of international jurists in clarifying complex and sometimes ambiguous treaties.

There is a specific meaning of the term 'suppressed' in a broad ecclesiastical application. For example, in the Papal Constitution *Regimini Ecclesiae Universae* of 15 August 1967, Pope Paul VI suppressed many institutions, secretariats and chancelleries in the course of reforming the Curia. His Holiness used the term 'suppressed' to mean that he removed the independent existence of a particular institution and handed its activities or duties to another, usually larger institution, such as the Secretariat of State or the Prefecture of the Pontifical Household, which in future would carry out those functions. The best example is that mentioned in Part I, the Chancellery of the Pontifical Equestrian Orders, which was assigned to the Secretariat of State, and the duties of its Grand Chancellor were — though not expressly — transferred to the Cardinal Secretary of State *pro tempore*. The Secretariat of State has always had a *Commissione per le Onorificenze*, a permanent Commission dealing with papal honours whose responsibility is in the field of ecclesiastical honours and promotions of Prelates. However, the administration of the Pontifical Equestrian Orders is also the responsibility of the Secretariat of State.

All other Catholic-founded Orders of Knighthood are linked to sovereign countries or Heads of legitimate non-regnant Royal Houses who have retained their links with the Holy See which continues to recognise their dynastic status and privilege to confer the Catholic Dynastic Orders of the Royal House. Their interests are also looked after by the Secretariat of State.

It was for this reason that the task of gathering information and compiling a compendium of the Catholic-founded Orders of Knighthood was delegated to a number of experts who worked with Archbishop Cardinale for many years. Several experts died during the lifetime of Mgr. Cardinale, and the Archbishop's untimely death in 1983, followed shortly afterwards by the death of the two remaining active collaborators in the Secretariat of State, was to a large extent the reason why the mantle of responsibility for producing an extensively revised and enlarged edition of *Orders of Knighthood, Awards and the Holy See*, published in October 1985, was placed on my shoulders.

Before going further in explaining some of the complex difficulties I had to deal with, I must, once again, set the record straight. Either for purposes of flattery or, perhaps, to lend weight to something which had been said in the 1985 edition, I found myself being credited with "speaking for the Holy See". My brief has never been to speak *for* the Holy See; my task has always been clearly defined: I was to express clearly and unambiguously the Holy See's views on, and attitude to, Catholic-founded Orders of Knighthood and Awards of Merit and endeavour to revise and improve on *"this compendium of facts which hitherto could only be found in scattered and hard-to-find sources"*. These are the actual words of His Holiness Pope John Paul II, which His Eminence Cardinal Casaroli, the Secretary of State, very graciously conveyed to me.

The expression 'scattered and hard-to-find sources' was an accurate description of fact. Both Part I of this book, which deals with the Pontifical Equestrian Orders, and Part II which deals with matters arising out of the publication of *Orders of Knighthood, Awards and the Holy See*, are largely based on such sources and the diligent work of jurists in defining them. This, however, was only made possible by the exacting task of the translators of many documents.

Much insight can be gained from observing traditions, or listening to those whose work in the Holy See spans a life time. The phrase *'sequitur'*, 'it follows therefore', perhaps made as a casual remark during a conversation, can lead to an unexpected discovery of corroborative evidence one had missed when it was seen out of context.

The main problems concerning Catholic and Catholic-founded Orders of Knighthood referred to, as already stated, the terms 'suppressed', 'abolished' and 'extinct'.

CHAPTER TWO

SUPPRESSION AND ABOLITION OF A CATHOLIC ORDER OF KNIGHTHOOD

An Order of Knighthood became a *Catholic* Order through bilateral institution, either jointly by Papal Brief and Royal Letters Patent, or when following its temporal legal foundation, the sovereign Head of the Order asked the Supreme Pontiff for a Papal Brief to confirm and approve the Order. In both instances such Orders of Knighthood have always been considered bilaterally established Orders. The Papal Brief also added a universal dimension to a national institution.

A Catholic Order of Knighthood can only become extinct when it has been abolished bilaterally by Papal Brief and Royal Letters Patent or if, in exceptional circumstances, the Holy See were to withdraw the appellation *Catholic* from the Order and to expressly condemn and abolish it. The mere withdrawal of the appellation *Catholic* from an Order of Knighthood does not imply that the Holy See withdraws its recognition from the Order after it has been secularised. (Orders in this category can be found in Chapter Ten in *Orders of Knighthood, Awards and the Holy See*).

Unilateral suppression of a Catholic Order is the legitimate prerogative of a sovereign nation. The suppression, however, is strictly confined to the territory of the country of foundation, and the Order does not become extinct but, according to International Law, continues to flourish outside the country.

When the suppression of a Catholic Order of Knighthood becomes the subject of a dispute, the legal aspects and, sometimes, the political consequences become very complex.

Because of his arbitrary use of the terms 'suppressed' and 'abolished' and his placement of some Orders in Chapter Nine, 'Extinct Catholic Orders of Knighthood', Archbishop Cardinale, quite unintentionally, brought to the surface some problems which needed a solution. I do not wish to give the impression that it would have been possible to shirk the responsibility for the restoration of an Order of Knighthood — declared extinct by Mgr. Cardinale — to the list of extant Orders, because that was the second of fourteen priorities I was given in 1983.

I gained my first expreience in this field with an Order I knew very little about, and what I knew was wrong because the illustration of the decoration indicated that it was a Polish Order which had ceased being *Catholic* in 1831 when the Russian Empire had annexed it.

The Catholic-founded Polish Equestrian Order of the White Eagle had been placed among the extinct Orders because the Polish Ambassador to Bruxelles had informed Archbishop Cardinale that: "The Order of the White Eagle has ceased to exist because the Parliament of the Polish People's Republic has passed a law abolishing it".

Because of the Order's history and its reconstitution as Poland's highest honour in 1921, after the new Republic of Poland had come into being in 1918, the protest from the very large Polish community resident outside Poland was understandably strong.

Several factors contributed to this issue, threatening considerable embarrassment: the Poles are among the most loyal Catholics in the world, and even under Communist rule, Poland has remained a predominantly Catholic nation. I knew that representations and strong protests had been made to His Holiness, but that the Pope had felt unable to comment, let alone intervene, on a subject he was not familiar with. On my return to England, I came to appreciate the full extent of the bitterness felt by the Poles, because they linked the extinction of the Order of the White Eagle with an action taken in 1972 by Pope Paul VI, who had the envoys of the Polish Government-in-exile — accredited to the Holy See since 1939 — removed from the list of active diplomats; Pope Paul is said to have done so to facilitate a diplomatic exchange with the Polish People's Republic. At the time of writing, fifteen years later, no such exchange has materialised. Many eminent Poles felt betrayed by the Holy See for declaring the Order of the White Eagle extinct. In fairness to the Holy See, especially Pope John Paul II and Cardinal Casaroli, the Secretary of State, they were taken by complete surprise by the matter which aroused such strong feelings; they had not even had the time to read the Archbishop Cardinale's book when the protests came pouring in.

On pages 188/9 and Colour Plate XX of the 1985 edition of *Orders of Knighthood, Awards and the Holy See* I was able to show that the Catholic Equestrian Order of the White Eagle of Poland had not been abolished but merely suppressed in the Polish People's Republic.

As a result of many hours of research and work with international jurists, I learned another, very important lesson for future research: the principles on which International Law is based are very simple and they usually confirm the obvious.

Although the sovereignty of a nation must not be curbed or restricted by another sovereign power, when one sovereign power enters into a partnership with another, that partnership may be terminated unilaterally, but the object of the partnership remains inviolable outside the territory of the partner terminating the agreement.

The Order of the White Eagle was constituted by Royal letters Patent by King Augustus II of Poland in 1705 and by Papal Brief of Pope Clement XI.

I felt greatly relieved, however, that the dispute about the Order of the White Eagle was resolved by the jurists without having to involve the Holy See as a partner to an agreement that had been unilaterally broken. The Government of the Polish People's Republic had made available to me an English translation of the law passed by the Polish Parliament on 17 February 1960. Article 29 of the Bill of which, quoted as the relevant passage abolishing the Order of the White Eagle, was unanimously declared by the jurists to have no other effect on the Order than to prohibit in future the award of that Order in Poland. Legally, Article 29 did not even constitute an express suppression of the Order but could only be interpreted as placing the Order of the White Eagle in abeyance in the Polish People's Republic.

Had it not been for the dispute about the Order of the White Eagle, another, far rarer, example of the laws governing the conferment of a Catholic-founded Order would never have become known.

The history of the Noble Order of the Golden Fleece is well documented, and both the Austrian and the Spanish branches of the Order have restained their Catholic dynastic character, though the criteria of conferment between the two branches differ greatly. Similarly the Supreme Order of Christ, the highest Pontifical Equestrian Order, and the Military Order of Christ of Portugal have a common origin. Today they are conferred by different grantors in different countries.

The conferment of an Order by two grantors is therefore not without precedent, nor is the conferment of an Order on the same person by two grantors; in 1983, H.R.H. The Grand Duke Jean of Luxembourg received the Order of the Golden Fleece of Spain from H.M. King Juan Carlos I, having already received the Austrian Golden Fleece from H.I. and R. H. Archduke Otto von Habsburg.

The second highest Polish Equestrian Order which was reconstituted in 1921 by the new Polish Republic was the Order of *Polonia Restituta*. However, because of the abuse of that Order during the years it had been annexed by Imperial Russia, the name of the Order was changed, though the ribbon and some characteristics of the Catholic-founded Order of St. Stanislaus had been retained. The Polish Government-in-exile continued to award of the Order of *Polonia Restituta* throughout the Second World War and afterwards under the constitution which acknowledged the bilateral foundation of the Order of St. Stanislaus by King Stanislaus Augustus in 1765 and by Papal Brief of Pope Clement XIII, and that the Order of *Polonia*

Restituta was the legitimate successor to the Catholic Order of St. Stanislaus; (see Appendix V, pages 315/6 in *Orders of Knighthood, Awards and the Holy See*).

In common with several Western nations, the Holy See recognises both the Order conferred by the Polish President-in-exile and the Order, constituted as an expressly secular Order by the polish People's Republic.

The Crosses of each Order differ slightly: that conferred by the Polish President-in-exile shows the white Polish eagle on the red medallion with a royal crown, and on the reverse medallion the year 1918; the Cross conferred by the Chairman of the Central Committee of the Communist Party in Poland shows the eagle without the crown and the medallion on the reverse bears the year 1944.

There is one question which will remain unanswered for the time being: Is the Order of *Polonia Restituta* which is conferred by the Polish President-in-exile and which has not changed its constitution and appearance since 1921 the same Order as that conferred in the Polish People's Republic, or are they different Orders bearing the same name?

CHAPTER THREE

CAN EXTINCT CATHOLIC ORDERS OF KNIGHTHOOD BECOME EXTANT?

The answer to the above question is 'no', provided, of course, that the Orders have been bilaterally abolished or fall into one of the other categories of Orders classified as extinct. However, if a Catholic Order of Knighthood has been listed as extinct because of a misunderstanding or a breakdown in communication or no communication at all between the owner of the Order and the institution or person responsible for the listing, there is no time limit which prevents the legitimate owner asking for the Order or Orders to be listed correctly.

Since *Orders of Knighthood, Awards and the Holy See* was first published on 25 March 1983, three Catholic Orders of Portugal have been listed as extinct. It was not until after the revised edition was published in October 1985 that I was approached by the representatives of H.R.H. Dom Duarte Pio, Duke of Braganza and Head of the Royal House of Portugal, asking to have these three Orders recognised extant as Catholic Dynastic Orders of Knighthood. To do this I had to follow a procedure which ensures that any amendment is not only founded on irrefutable proof but that it will cause no friction between the Holy See and the republican Government of Portugal.

A new regime rarely adopts former Dynastic Orders, the usual practice being to surpress them and institute new Orders and decorations of merit. Before I could do anything, I had therefore to satisfy myself on three counts, that: 1) H.R.H. Dom Duarte Pio, Duke of Braganza, was the legitimate Head of the Royal House of Portugal and successor to the last reigning Monarch, H.M. Dom Manuel II, who had reigned until 1910; 2) the Orders claimed as Catholic Dynastic Orders of Knighthood had always been the property of the House of Brangaza and had never belonged to the Crown of Portugal and therefore to the State, and consequently become the property of the republican Government after the Revolution of 1910; and finally, 3) I had to ascertain that there was no impediment on canonical grounds which would make an amendment impossible for any of the three Orders claimed.

In his reference to the Order of the Conception of Our Lady of Vila Viçosa, Archbishop Cardinale had not mentioned suppression; he had merely given a brief historical account of the Order. In the case of the Order of St. Isabel, he stated clearly that it had been suppressed by the republican Government after the Revolution of 1910. With regard to the third Order claimed as a Catholic Dynastic Order by the Duke of Braganza, the Order of St. Michael of the Wing, Mgr. Cardinale had introduced for the first and only time a canonical term which I assumed to be a serious obstacle to placing the Order among the extant Orders of Knighthood, the *Bullarium Romanum*.

It is inevitable that some subjects are repeated in different contexts; for example, in the chapter dealing with self-styled and fantasy orders, I deal in detail with organisations that are registered with an appropriate governmental department as charities or non-profit-making associations etc., but have no status as an Order of Chivalry. As far as the Portuguese Orders were concerned, they had been registered and their registration had been published in the official gazette the *DIARIO DA REPÚBLICA*.

I had to explain to the representatives of the Orders that such a gazetting was of little, if any, use to me because it neither proved chivalric status nor ownership. Instead, I suggested that it might be easier to adopt the normal procedure of claiming Dynastic Orders for a Royal House, whether or not the Orders had the appellation *'Catholic'*. I suggested that His Royal Highness should prepare and publish in Portugal a declaration claiming the three Orders of Knighthood as Dynastic Orders of the House of Braganza.

On 27 October 1986, H.R.H. Dom Duarte Pio, Duke and Head of the Royal House of Portugal issued a proclamation to that effect in Lisbon. I received a copy of this declaration with the courteous request to transfer the Dynastic Orders from the list of extinct Catholic Orders of Knighthood to the list of extant Orders at the earliest possible opportunity.

The Duke of Braganza further explained that the devotion of the Royal House of Braganza to the Holy Roman Catholic Church was recognised by Pope Benedict XIV in 1749 when His Holiness granted to the Sovereigns of Portugal the honour of the appellation *Most Faithful Majesty*.

Because of past experience, I considered it prudent to protect myself against possible allegations that — whatever the outcome of my research into the three Orders might be — it had not lacked the thoroughness essential to such an important investigation. To avoid any possible embarrassment, especially that I lacked academic thoroughness and care in obtaining the correct facts, which were made by by some Orders against Archbishop Cardinale, I took all possible precautions. I went considerably further in proofs I required before accepting them than Archbishop Cardinale had ever thought necessary or, indeed, had I, originally.

Before embarking on this additional burden, I informed the Order of St.

Michael of the Wing that, in the absence of a promoter of their cause who could prove to my satisfaction that Duke of Braganza's claim was justified, and the references to the *Bullarium Romanum*, which I feared might prove an unsurmountable obstacle to their aims, it might be better to postpone any research until a later date, as any negative result, once published, would jeopardise any future change.

Although the status of H.R.H. Dom Duarte Pio, Duke of Braganza, as Head of the Royal House was not in doubt, I had to have proof that: 1) that the royal proclamation, dated 27 October 1986, had been signed and sealed by him, and I needed a certified English translation of the contents; 2) the Duke of Braganza could legitimately claim these Orders, and that the Orders were not on the list of Orders of the Republic of Portugal; 3) the reference by Mgr. Cardinale to the *Bullarium Romanum* with regard to the Order of St. Michael of the Wing, did not preclude that Order from being eligible as a Catholic Order of Knighthood.

Before I received satisfactory independent replies to the first two questions, I was informed that Church authorities in New York had reported that a serious abuse of the Order of St. Michael of the Wing was being perpetrated, and the names of the Dukes of Braganza and Viseu and of others could be found in a 'catalogue', offering the Order for sale and asking for a US$2,000, entrance fee into the Order. I immediately postponed any further research and informed its representatives of the reason.

The prompt action by the Order of St. Michael of the Wing of Portugal and independent information which reached me within days from Rome, showing that similar abuses and misrepresentations had been perpetrated in the U.S.A. by the same persons with regard to legitimate Catholic Orders of Chivalry, persuaded me to continue the research and also find, if possible, an early answer to what still appeared to me an unsurmountable problem, the *Bullarium Romanum*.

Only if I were to be completely satisfied that all criteria had been met for transferring any one or all of the Portuguese Orders into the 'extant' category, would and could I do so.

131

HISTORIE
CRONOLOGICHE
D E L L' O R I G I N E
DEGL ORDINI MILITARI
E   D I   T V T T E

LE RELIGIONI CAVALLERESCHE
Infino ad hora inſtituite nel Mondo,

Inſegue, Croci , Stendardi , Habiti Capitolari , ò di Ceremonia,
Statuti , e Conſtituzioni di cadaun'Ordine .

Guerre Campali , e Nauali , Azioni , Fatti Celebri , & Impreſe de Caualieri ;
Confederazioni , Trattati , Paci, & auuenimenti per difeſa del Nome
Chriſtiano, e propagazione della Fede Cattolica.

SERIE DI TVTTI I PRENCIPI GRAN MAESTRI,
Ordini di Dame , e degl'Infedeli &c. Con le loro Diuiſe.

Naſra ## OPERA DELL' ABBATE *Sivra*
BERNARDO GIVSTINIAN
Caualiere Gran Croce nell'Ordine Imperiale di S. Giorgio , &c.

P A R T E   P R I M A.

IN VENEZIA,
Preſſo Combi, & LàNoù .
Con Licenza de' Superiori, e Priuilegio .
M DC XCII.

IS THE *BULLARIUM ROMANUM* PROOF THAT AN ORDER OF KNIGHTHOOD HAS BEEN FOUNDED OR APPROVED BY PAPAL BRIEF?

This is a question, which, to the best of my knowledge, has never been raised before. At least I have found no evidence for the *Bullarium Romanum* having been cited as proof concerning Orders of Knighthood. I do not know why Archbishop Cardinale mentioned it in his notes, or from whom, or where, he had obtained the information that the Portuguese Order was supposedly not listed in the *Bullarium Romanum*, thus casting by implication serious doubt on the Order ever having existed.

I had no option but to start a thorough research and ascertain the rôle and function of the *Bullarium Romanum* with regard to Orders of Knighthood in general and the Order of St. Michael of the Wing of Portugal in particular.

Bullarium is a term commonly applied to a collection of Papal Bulls, Papal Briefs and other analogous papal documents, whether the scope of the collection be general in character, or whether it be limited to the bulls connected with any particular Religious Order, Order of Knighthood, institution or locality. The name *Bullarium* seems to have been invented by the canonist Laertius Cherubini, who in 1586 published under the title *Bullarium sive Collectio diversarum Constitutionum multorum Pontificum* a large folio volume of 1404 pages containing 922 constitutions from Gregory VII down to the Pope then reigning, Sixtus V.

With regard to this and all subsequent collections, three things have carefully to be borne in mind. First, whatever may have been the intrinsic importance or binding force of any of the bulls so published, the selection itself was a matter which depended entirely upon the arbitrary choice of various editors. As a collection the publication had no official character. The only recognised exception to this assertion is the first volume of a collection of his own bulls which was sent by Pope Benedict XIV in 1746 to the University of Bologna to serve as a *fons iuris*, or source of legal principles. Secondly, it was never seriously maintained, despite some rather pretentious title pages, that these collections were in any sense complete or that they even included all the constitutions of more general interest. Thirdly, it was the intention of the editors, at least at first, rather to exclude than to include papal pronouncements which had already been incorporated in the text of the Canon Law or some other official collection of papal documents. The object of the early collections was to render assistance to canonists by bringing within their reach papal enactments which either had been overlooked by the compilers of the *Corpus* or which had been issued subsequent to the latest decrees included in it.

There are about twenty major *Bullaria Romana*, some containing over thirty volumes: the most famous are 'The Luxembourg Bullarium', Mainardi's *Roman Bullarium* and the 'Turin Bullarium'. In addition there exist countless 'Particular Bullaria' which, as the general title suggests, deal exclusively with one specific religious or chivalric Order. Historically speaking, the most interesting Papal Bulls, Briefs and documents are often those contained in the *Regesta* which have never been included in the general *Bullaria*.

It may be added that many compendiums to the *Bullaria Romana* were published, particularly in the eighteenth century, and many commentaries have been published in the seventeenth and eighteenth century.

I freely confess to much ignorance on the subject of the *Bullaria Romana*; I believed that there was one *Bullarium*, perhaps in several volumes, and the only reason I approached the Vatican Archives was to arrange a convenient time when I could have a look at them to check Archbishop Cardinale's notes which I had subsequently published as a footnote to the article on the Portuguese Order *de São Miguel da Ala*, of St. Michael of the Wing, in the section on the 'extinct Catholic Orders', (1985 edition of *Orders of Knighthood, Awards and the Holy See*, page 187).

I first familiarised myself with the work by Fr. Herbert Thurston, S. J., who had written a comprehensive treatise on the *Bullarium Romanum*.

To my surprise I also found several works dealing in some detail with the Order of St. Michael of the Wing, but I saw from the notes I had been sent by the Order before I began my research that most of them were known to the House of Braganza and to the Order. I even had been sent photocopies of some relevant sections. The most interesting of these books was one by Abbot D. Ascanio Tamburinio, published in 1691, because it had all the hallmarks of a *Bullarium Romanum*. It is, in fact, classified as one of the 'Particular Bullaria' because it contains the Papal Briefs of successive Popes concerning the Orders which are listed under 'Monastic Military Orders' in *Orders of Knighthood, Awards and the Holy See* (pp. 160–164). In Abbot Tamburinio's *De Iure Abbatum et Aliorum Praelatorum etc.*, Volume II, (pages 418–419) are Papal Briefs of Alexander VII and of Clement IX, concerning the Orders of Alcantara, Calatrava, Alfama, Montesa and *Ordo Equitum S. Michaelis sive de Ala*, the Order of St. Michael of the Wing.

Another useful source of information proved to be the *Histoire*

Chronologiche dell'Origine degl'Ordini Militari e di Tutte le Religioni Cavalleresche by the Abbot Bernardo Giustiniani, himself a Knight Grand Cross of the Constantinian Order of St. George, published in 1692 in Venice. It is an encyclopedic work, and Part I contains the *Serie de' Maestri, ò Gran Maestri dell'Ordine di S. Michiele in Portogallo*. A list of the Cavalieri dell'Ala di S. Michiele in Portogallo appears on pages 428–433, and on page 431 is the complete list of the first twenty-three Grand Masters of the Order, their date of appointment and the years of their reigns. This work was first published in 1672, the same year Elias Ashmole published *The Institution, Laws & Ceremonies of the Most Noble Order of the Garter*, which mentions (Chapter II, page 70) The Order of the Wing of St. Michael in Portugal among the Religious Orders of Knighthood. Ashmole also states that the Knights belonged to the Religious Order of the Cistercians and followed the rule of St. Benedict; their main task was defending the Catholic Religion, defending the borders of the country against the invading Moors, and bringing comfort and relief to widows and the fatherless.

Ashmole's last sentence is of great interest: he states that the Order has fallen into disuse, but that the Grandmastership of the Order has firmly remained with the Kings of Portugal, implying that the Order had been placed temporarily in abeyance. However, he does not expressly say so.

Corroborative evidence of the Order's Monastic-Military character can be found in part I of the *Cistercian Chronicles* compiled between 1597 and 1602 by the Cistercian D. Fr. Bernardo de Britto of the Abbey of Alcobaça, published in 1720 on behalf of His Majesty the King of Portugal. Knights of the Order of St. Michael of the Wing owed their allegiance to the Abbot of Alcobaça. Fr. Bernardo de Britto also chronicles the legendary aspects of the Order's foundation, and I gained the distinct impression that, unintentionally, the Chronicler of Alcobaça sowed the seeds of a misunderstanding, especially abroad, because he himself appears to be unsure of the correct interpretation of the 'Wing" of St. Michael. Although in the Constitution of the Order, published by the Order of the Cistercians in 1630 the name is given in Latin as *Constitutiones Militum S. Michaelis sive de ALA*, Fr. Bernardo de Britto repeats a confusing linguistic element in the chronicles. Referring to this Cistercian Order of St. Michael, he describes it in Portuguese as *"da Ala, ou Asa"*, in the introductory section of Chapter XVIII, and from then on arbitrarily as *Ala* and *Asa*.

The difference is a subtle one: in Portuguese *Ala* is a supportive wing, such as a wing in the army, which is employed in a specific strategic rôle during a battle; *Asa* is the wing of a bird, or of an angel. Because the emblem of the Order has always been a wing, and because of the legendary stories surrounding the Order's foundation, later publications, especially foreign ones, opted for the anatomical rather than the strategic wing when giving the name of the Order. The English word 'wing' can mean either.

The *Bullarium Romanum* has been of little help apart from the the Papal Brief of Alexander VII in *Iure Abbatum et Aliorum Praelatorum etc.*, which some scholars place among the Particular Bullaria because it states on the title page that it contains *Conciliorum, Sacrorum Canonum, Constitutionum Pontificum Authoritate etc.* All important Religious Orders had at one time or other in the seventeenth and eighteenth centuries collected all Papal Briefs concerning their privileges and published them. The collection of the Cistercians (1691) is no exception.

As far as the Order of St. Michael of the Wing is concerned, details about it are in one of the "Particular *Bullaria Romana*", and additional information proved beyond any doubt that the Order flourished, was placed in abeyance, recalled from abeyance and for some time used as a political movement, but always strictly adhering to its foremost task: the defence of the faith of the Holy Roman Church against modernism and liberalism. The Order was suppressed by the branch of the Royal Family which embraced modernism and liberalism but was supported by the branch which fought for the rights of the Holy Catholic Church, until in 1932 that branch of the Braganza family became the heir to the Headship of the Royal House of Braganza.

Throughout its chequered history, the Order's Grandmastership was always vested in the legitimate Head of the Royal House of Portugal. Certain purists maintain that a non-regnant successor to a Sovereign can only claim those Dynastic Orders which were Dynastic Orders at the time of the last Sovereign. This is correct, and no Head of as Royal House who is not a Sovereign can create a new Order of Knighthood.

The Grandmastership of the Order of St. Michael of the Wing has at all times remained with the Sovereigns of Portugal. The fact that some chose not to confer the Order is legally irrelevant. At no time was the Order of St. Michael of the Wing abolished. The period when the Order was regarded as a 'secret society' for the defence of traditional principles of the Holy Roman Church, fighting against modernism and liberalism which was rampant in parts of the Royal House, has no bearing on the Order's chivalric status either. The fact that the Grandmastership of the Order has remained with the Head of the House of Braganza has guaranteed the Order's continued existence.

The proof with regard to the Order of St. Michael of the Wing rested on two factors: first, it had to be shown that the *Bullarium Romanum* was not an obstacle, secondly, the Grandmastership of the Order had to be shown to have remained with the head of the House of Braganza. The latter point would also prove the legitimacy of the Duke's claim.

The many volumes which make up the *Bullarium Romanum* are important and useful when used as corroborative evidence, but it would be unwise to attribute to them more influence than that.

DE
JURE
ABBATUM,
ET ALIORUM
PRÆLATORUM,
Tàm Regularium, quàm Secularium
EPISCOPIS INFERIORUM,
TOMUS SECUNDUS;
IN QUO DE EORUM POTESTATE
Spirituali in univerfum, præfertim qucad Pontificalia, & Ec-
clefiæ Sacramenta, ac Sacramentalia, Ecclefiafticas cenfuras, & omnia,
tam folennia, quàm fimplicia Vota, copiosè
differitur:

CONCILIORUM, SACRORUM CANONUM,
Conftitutionum Pontificum Authoritate: necnon
SS. Patrum Sententiis, Legulatorum Regularis Difciplina Regulis, & omnium
Religionum Decretis, Theologorum, & Jurisdivoutium Placitis, juxta Romana
Curia Praxim illuftratos.

Accedunt Congregationum omnium, tam Regularium,
quàm Secularium, & Militarium, in quatuor præcipuis Regulis SS. Bafilii,
Auguftini, Benedicti, & Francifci militantium, & Equeftrium Ordinum Secularum,
nulli peculiari Regula addictorum, Inftitutiones.

AUTHORE
D. ASCANIO TAMBURINIO
DE MARRADIO, S·T·M· ABBATE PASSINIA-
nenfi, Congregationis Vallis-Umbrofæ: olim ejusdem Congregationis
Generali, Sereniffimi Principis Cardinalis Caroli Medicæ à facris
Confultationibus.

Poft tres quæ in Gallia prodierunt Editiones prima in Germania auctior & corre-
ctior, neceffariis indicibus illuftrata.

Cum Privilegio Sacræ Cæfareæ Majeftatis.

COLONIÆ AGRIPPINÆ,
Apud JOANNEM BALTHASAREM COOMANS.
Typis JOANNIS PHILIPPI ANDREÆ·
M. DC. XCI.

137

CHAPTER FIVE

CATHOLIC ORDERS OF KNIGHTHOOD AND AWARDS IN ABEYANCE

Catholic Orders of Knighthood or Awards of Merit which had been placed in abeyance were not given a separate chapter in *Orders of Knighthood, Awards and the Holy See*. In fact, it is fair to say that this field is one of grey areas where no guidelines exist.

In retrospect I can say that the title of Chapter Five, "Religious but not Pontifical Awards recognised by the Holy See", is a misnomer. None of the three Awards mentioned is awarded at present. Pope Pius XII issued a statement in the *Acta Apostolicae Sedis* and in *L'Osservatore Romano* in 1954 that the Lateran Cross was not a Pontifical Award, although it had assumed the title 'Papal Lateran Cross', and he instructed those who awarded it so lavishly to cease awarding the Cross.

The same applied to the Lauretan Cross. In both cases Pope Leo XIII had sanctioned or given his *nihil obstat* to their institution.

The Archbasilica of St. John Lateran and the adjoining Palace are the centre of the administration of the Vicariat of Rome, and it was the Chapter of the Canons of the Archbasilica who bestowed on benefactors the Lateran Cross in gold, silver or bronze.

Similarly, the Lauretan Cross, which was approved by Leo XIII in 1888, was a privilege granted to the Bishop or Delegate of the Holy House of Loreto to confer on benefactors in gold, silver and bronze.

Although Pope Pius XII did not expressly place the Orders in abeyance or abolish them, acts which are the prerogative of the Supreme Pontiff alone in cases of Pontifical and Religious Orders and Awards, such as ordering the conferment to cease, is at the very least an act placing the two Awards in abeyance. It would need a Papal Brief from one of the Pope's successors to allow the conferment to resume.

In the case of the Lateran Cross, the placing of the Cross in abeyance by the Supreme Pontiff was preceded by several severe warnings to the .conferring Chapter by the Papal Secretariat of State.

The third Award in Chapter Five, 'The Holy Land Pilgrim's Cross', which in its diverse forms belonged to the Equestrian Order of the Holy Sepulchre, was not placed in abeyance but replaced by two new Awards of Merit. These and the Cross of Merit of the Order are the only 'Religious but not Pontifical

Awards' in existence at the present time, and details about them can be found in Part III, the Addenda to the Chapter on the Equestrian Order of the Holy Sepulchre of Jerusalem.*

The question as to who may place Catholic Dynastic Orders in abeyance can be answered without qualification: only the Head of the Royal House to whom the Dynastic Order belongs can place it in abeyance. It means the temporary suspension of the conferment of the Order, and it is an internal matter for the Royal House to resolve. If, however, the Head of the Royal House intends placing a Catholic Dynastic Order into abeyance beyond his own life time because he wishes to see the Order conferred subject to specific conditions, it would be necessary to use the same laws which apply to a bilateral abolition, with the proviso that the Order is not abolished so as to become extinct, and that it should continue to exist but may not be conferred until and unless both a legitimate Head of the Royal House and the Holy See agree that the specific conditions required for a conferment are fulfilled.

In 1979, H.R.H. Prince Henri, Count of Orléans and Head of the Royal House of Bourbon-Orléans, informed Archbishop Cardinale that the Catholic Dynastic Orders of his Royal House should only be conferred by reigning Sovereigns and not by Heads of the Royal House who were not regnant. The three Orders are: The Order of the Holy Ghost, The Royal and Military Order of St. Louis and the Order of St. Michael of France. Archbishop Cardinale took note of the wishes of His Royal Highness and added an appropriate footnote to the section dealing with the Dynastic Orders of the Royal House of Bourbon-Orléans.

I shall return to this point at the end of this chapter. Early in 1987, I was handed a photocopy of a letter signed by Philippe Duc de Württemberg, asking on behalf of his brother-in-law Archduke Gottfried, Head of the Royal House of Habsburg-Tuscany, for the Dynastic Orders of the Royal House, the Order of St. Joseph and the Order of St. Stephen, to be placed in abeyance because both Orders were being abused by imposters.

All I could do was to consult *unofficially* a member of the Papal Secretariat of State in March 1987 and ask for guidance. He pointed out to me that apart from the fact that the original letter was dated 27 April 1973, ten years before Archbishop Cardinale's death, only the Head of a Royal House could place its Dynastic Orders in abeyance. Also, he produced a reference book which showed that there was now a new Head of the Royal House of Bourbon-Tuscany, a successor to Archduke Gottfried, in fact, even

---

* Both the Sovereign Military Order of Malta and the Equestrian Order of the Holy Sepulchre of Jerusalem, award their own distinct and highly esteemed Orders of Merit. The Order *Pro Merito Melitensi* and The Order of Merit. Both Orders are awarded in classes equivalent to ranks in Orders of Knighthood.

when Archduke Gottfried was still alive, Philippe Duc de Württemberg could not have placed, or requested to have placed the Orders in abeyance for his brother-in-law.

The Prelate suggested that I had probably been given the photocopy to publish the letter, thus creating the impression that it was the Holy See's view that the Order of St. Joseph and the Order of St. Stephen of the Royal House of Habsburg-Tuscany had been placed in abeyance. However well intended this may have been, the fact that the Royal House has a new Head and that the photocopy was fourteen years old, made it in any case superfluous.

He returned then to the information H.R.H. Prince Henri, Count of Paris and Head of the Royal House of Bourbon-Orléans had conveyed to Archbishop Cardinale, who in 1979 was, apart from being Apostolic Nuncio to Belgium and to Luxembourg, the Apostolic Nuncio to the European Community, (appointed on 10 November 1970).

Although Mgr. Cardinale had appended a footnote to the appropriate section in the book, expressing the opinion of His Royal Highness, Mgr. Cardinale knew that such a footnote did not constitute an act of placing three Orders in abeyance. Had His Royal Highness approached the Apostolic Nuncio to France with the request to place before the Secretariat of State of His Holiness his wish to have the support of the Holy See in placing the three Orders in abeyance until they could be conferred again by a reigning Sovereign of France, his wish would have been granted if the Secretary of State had shared the sentiments of His Royal Highness.

Not every request to have a Catholic Dynastic Order placed temporarily in abeyance would incorporate the requirement that conferment of that Order be reserved to á reigning Sovereign. There could be other, valid reasons. If the Secretary of State shared those views, the Order could, indeed, be placed in abeyance bilaterally, and any future Head of the Royal House would have to request the Holy See, through the Secretary of State, to restore the right of conferment before the Order could be conferred again.

The Holy See, *Mater et Magistra* of all Catholic-founded Orders of Knighthood, would protect the Order against abuse, false claimants or imposters from reviving the Order while it was in the bilaterally agreed abeyance.

My personal opinion is that such a procedure would be reasonably simple to implement if a Head of a Royal House wished to place a Catholic Dynastic Order in abeyance while providing the best possible security for the Order's continued existence. However, I cannot state forcefully enough that once an Order has been bilaterally abolished, it cannot be revived or recalled from extinction.

At the date of publication of *The Cross on the Sword* the only two decorations or awards in abeyance are the Lateran Cross and the Lauretan Cross. The three Dynastic Orders of the House of Bourdon-Orléans are temporarily not conferred but they are not in abeyance.

As stated at the beginning of this chapter, we are dealing with a grey area of chivalric procedure. Only a Pontifical Tribunal could recommend procedures to the Supreme Pontiff which, if accepted, would become binding on all Royal Houses which have Catholic Dynastic Orders.

CHAPTER SIX

SELF-STYLED ORDERS

From the start, most complaints were received from those organisations that are listed in Chapter Eleven of *Orders of Knighthood, Awards and the Holy See* as self-styled orders of chivalry. As far as these organisations are concerned, there has been no change in the attitude of the Holy See.

As I received many letters from members of orders styled 'of St. Lazarus of Jerusalem', it looked at times as if there was a concerted attempt to put pressure on me. I therefore wrote to the Cardinal Secretary of State, explaining the situation and asking for guidance as to whether a review of the status of these orders should be contemplated. An immediate written reply informed me that no review of such orders would ever be contemplated, now or in the future. I must therefore lay to rest all hopes of the orders of St. Lazarus of Jerusalem ever gaining any recognition from the Holy See, let alone receiving its approval.

Members of the clergy who have written to the Papal Secretariat of State, to me and even to the British Orders and Medals Research Society about any of the self-styled orders criticising the Holy See's uncompromising stand, especially on the orders styled 'of St. Lazarus of Jerusalem', are advised to read page 237 of *Orders of Knighthood, Awards and the Holy See*. This particular section was originally written at the request of Pope Paul VI for a different publication, but its tenor was strengthened by the Secretary of State to Pope John Paul II because the Holy See has become increasingly aware that misguided priests, and even some high dignitaries of the Church have lent their support to these organisations and accepted their decorations.

It has never been suggested that some of these organisations do not engage in commendable works of charity, but they do so as registered charities, or as limited companies or non-profit-making associations, and not as Orders of Knighthood recognised by the Holy See. Most of these self-styled orders continue to claim in their publicity brochures 'ipso facto' recognition by the Holy See. There is no such thing as 'ipso facto' recognition; the literal translation of the Latin is: 'by this fact'. The fact or facts which are supposed to have secured many self-styled orders recognition either range from the ridiculous to the pathetic, or are to be found in fraudulent or invalid documents, which exist only in photocopies. On occasion, a letter from a gullible ecclesiastical dignitary is produced, though he is most likely blissfully ignorant of the use which is being made of his letter.

For example, cardinals and high members of the Roman Curia are frequently asked for letters of introduction to Apostolic Nuncios abroad. I do not know what reasons Their Eminences and Excellencies are given for the need of such letters, but if some of them knew for what purpose their letters have been used, it would have Their Eminences and Excellencies in a perpetual state of agitation that they might one day find themselves accused of having aided and abetted activities of which the Holy See thoroughly disapproves.

There is a recent example: in a letter of introduction to an Apostolic Nuncio abroad, a Roman Cardinal gave to the petitioner all the possible titles of nobility the petitioner claimed to possess. Within days that person made an appointment to see the Apostolic Nuncio who, to his surprise was asked to confirm on the letter of introduction that it had been presented to him. Somehow he complied with this strange request and even added the seal of the Apostolic Nunciature to his signature. As soon as the visitor had left, the Nuncio had second thoughts about this unusual request, the first of its kind in his forty years service as a diplomat of the Holy See. He wrote a brief memorandum on the incident, attached a photocopy of the letter of introduction and sent it to the Secretariat of State in case intelligence from elsewhere might throw a further light on the episode. The Nuncio did not have to wait very long before he learned from friends and acquaintances that with photocopies of the letter of introduction bearing his endorsement, the person had gained entry into society, and shortly afterwards he read in the newspapers that illustrious titles of nobility where being offered for sale and worthless knighthoods bestowed on eager recipients. The person claimed, and probably still does, that the endorsement of the Cardinal's letter by the Apostolic Nuncio constituted not only 'ipso facto' recognition of all the titles of nobility by the 'Vatican' (where the letter was written) but also in the country to which the Apostolic Nuncio was accredited.

I have lost count of the number of self-styled Imperial, Royal and Serene Highnesses, Grand Masters, Supreme Commanders and Grand Chancellors of self-styled orders who have written to me since 1983 when it became known that I was to be the *Revisore* of *Orders of Knighthood, Awards and the Holy See*. I was commanded, ordered, threatened and begged to include them and their self-styled orders in the next edition or any subsequent supplement.

On one occasion, the publishers were offered substantial financial inducements if they would instruct their printers to omit the name of one particular organisation in Chapter Eleven. In 1985 an approach was made to them by an American publisher, offering an unrealistically high cash payment in advance on condition that I would waive my stipulation that an undertaking had to be sworn before a judge in New York, that no additions or deletions would be made to the American edition without my prior written consent, the penalty for any breach of which being very severe. It emerged a few weeks later that three self-styled orders of chivalry operating in, and from, the United States of America had joined forces and offered the U.S. publisher an immediate purchase order for 50,000 copies of the book provided some minor alterations with regard to the presentation of their organisations in the book were made.

In my opinion the activities of some 'knightly' organisations border on the criminal. They usually create for themselves a pseudo-respectable front behind which they carry out their less respectable trade. There is a distinct pattern to their operations: they use, without authority, the names of the Pontifical Equestrian Orders, the Sovereign Military Order of Malta, the Equestrian Order of the Holy Sepulchre of Jerusalem, and British Royal Orders, such as the Most Venerable Order of St. John, and they claim that their association is mainly composed of members of these Orders. They make membership conditional on belonging to a respectable Order of Knighthood and on being armigerous. The small-scale self-styled order has given way to a new phenomenon: the mail-order business. A catalogue offers a variety of 'respectable' orders for sale, and those lacking a coat of arms are invited to turn to the page where the organiser's own college of arms can oblige them with armorial bearings. However, the first obligation of the potential knight is the payment of a fee to join an order as a candidate. This fee can range from a modest $1,000. to $10,000., according to the prestige that respectable order holds. Coats of arms also vary in price, depending on what the client would like. Then follows a list of ranks, from a knight to a knight grand cross and even a collar. The candidate has a choice of the degree of respectability he can purchase in order to impress everyone at the next social function he goes to. However, although the candidate may be spending tens of thousands of dollars to get a rank in a certain order, he is reminded that there will be annual oblations which have to be paid promptly. There are further incentives: those joining a particular order, usually one that imitates the Sovereign Military Order of Malta, and who purchase and appropriate rank (with insignia and robes), are able to buy a "diplomatic" passport.

The "diplomatic" passports are more prevelant in some States in the U.S.A. than in others, but they are mainly used by their overbearing owners to claim diplomatic immunity when stopped for speeding or some other traffic offence. There are at present some fifty cases of bogus diplomatic passports being heard in County Courts in the United States of America, but according to reliable legal sources, for every holder of a bogus diplomatic passport who gets caught by an alert sheriff, fifty do not get a fine from the patrolman, but a respectful salute!

The organisers of the order business adorn themselves with appropriate titles and ranks in chivalric orders. Many style themselves 'Sir', and their post-nominal letters are identical to those of legitimate Orders of Knighthood.

There have been several attempts to bring the most audacious of these purveyors of 'honours' to court. Unfortunately, the laws of very few countries are adequate to deal with them. They have also amassed enough money to pay the finest legal brains to find loopholes in the law and so protect them from successful prosecutions.

If, on rare occasions, the opportunity offers itself to challenge one of the main operators, one can but marvel at the cleverness with which they manage to evade making an admission of fraud. A major operator who claimed to be a leading figure in the Equestrian Order of the Holy Sepulchre of Jerusalem, an Order of Knighthood under the direct protection of the Holy See, also used the post-nominal letters of that Order; having styled himself a G.C.H.S., a Knight Grand Cross of the Order of the Holy Sepulchre of Jerusalem, he was confronted with the evidence that he was not even a Roman Catholic and therefore could not possibly belong to the Order of which he claimed to be a Knight Grand Cross. He immediately produced a document which created him a Knight Grand Cross in the "Byzantine" Order of the Holy Sepulchre, a self-styled Order nobody had heard of. But he used this particular Order merely to be able to give himself respectability with post-nominal letters which are associated with the Roman Catholic Order.

Even more astonishing was the defence of a 'knight' who claimed for himself the appellation "Sir" before his name and the impressive post-nominal letters K.C.B., besides many more letters of self-styled Orders. K.C.B. is a Knight Commander of the Most Honourable Order of the Bath, the third highest ranking British Order of Knighthood which entitles the bearer to be called "Sir". However, when faced with the evidence that he was neither British nor a Knight Commander of the Bath and therefore not entitled to be called "Sir", he put up a brilliant defence: he had committed no deception whatever; he called himself by the ancient address of "Sir Knight". As nobody had been put on trial as yet for splitting an infinitive in a sentence, so all he was guilty of — if guilt was the right word — was splitting two nouns. He had placed the word 'Sir' before his Christian Name, and Knight after his surname in the form of the letters K.C.B. which, incidentally did in his case not stand for Knight Commander of the Bath, but for the Hospitaller Order of the Brothers of Burgos of which he was a Knight Commander. In American law, there is no case to answer, and I doubt whether any country has adequate laws against deceptions of this sort.

A recent mail-order brochure for bogus orders featured the coat of arms of Pope John Paul II on the front and the announcement that this organisation had just received the Apostolic Blessing of His Holiness Pope John Paul II on its good works!

Anyone believing that these order merchants are naive people suffering from megalomania should think again. These purveyors of self-styled orders are wily and accomplished salesmen, trading on the most vulnerable of human weaknesses: vanity. They are able to operate with impunity because they know that the laws in most countries are totally inadequate to stop them.

Those who are still in any doubt are strongly recommended to read *Orders & contre-ordres de chevalerie* by A. Chaffanjon & B. G. Flavigny, Paris 1982.

Hyginus Eugene Cardinale

Orders of Knighthood, Awards and the Holy See

Edited and revised
by
Peter Bander van Duren

PART III

Part III contains a section with *Errata* to the 1985 edition of *Orders of Knighthood, Awards and the Holy See*, and several *Addenda*. The latter are in separate chapters in the same order as, and with references to their place in, the book (which is in this part referred to by the letters OKAHS) and page number.

Arising out of the *Errata*, the first chapter deals with the Most Venerable Order of St. John (Great Britain) which is briefly mentioned in a corollary to The Sovereign Military Order of Malta, (OKAHS p. 91).

Continuing with the Religious Orders of Knighthood, the second Chapter gives additional information on the Equestrian Order of the Holy Sepulchre of Jerusalem, (OKAHS pp. 92–106).

Chapter Three deals with Dynastic Orders of Knighthood, and following some of the Addenda, is a chapter dealing with the House of Braganza, the Royal House of Portugal, which has been added to the Catholic Dynastic Orders of Knighthood bestowed by a legitimate successor of a Sovereign and Head of a Royal Family, (OKAHS pp. 140–158).

In the context of section three, I must reiterate what I have said in a different context before: unless there has been proof of an error on the part of the author or the revisor in the 1985 edition of *Orders of Knighthood, Awards and the Holy See*, or new information has come to light which is not contrary to the Holy See's views and attitude expressed before, I cannot add anything, however strongly I have been urged to do so, that would introduce points of view held by those who disagree with the attitude of the Holy See. This would also be contrary to the concept of both *Orders of Knighthood, Awards and the Holy See* and this supplementary volume, the purpose of which is to reflect the Holy See's views and attitude.

ERRATA TO *ORDERS OF KNIGHTHOOD, AWARDS AND THE HOLY SEE:*

p. 86: The Most Venerable Order of St. John was incorrectly described as ". . . the Protestant counterpart of the Sovereign Military Order of Malta. The Order of St. John is a Royal Order of Great Britain and open to all Christians as Members and, as Associates, to non-Christians. (See: Part III, Chapter One in this volume).

p. 104: The Cross of Merit of the Equestrian Order of the Holy Sepulchre of Jerusalem and the Holy Land Pilgrim's Cross (p. 106) have been reconstituted. (See Part III, Chapter Two in this volume).

p. 111: The Lateran Cross and Lauretan Cross are in abeyance. (See Part II, Chapter Five in this volume).

p. 147: Gaeta Medal: the ribbon *azzurro e bianco in palo* was reproduced wrongly. The ribbon was moiré with three stripes: sky-blue, white, sky-blue. A full-size medal in silver was sculpted by the papal Engraver, Rudolf Niedballa, KCSG.

p. 138: Abolition of the Order of St. Lazarus of Jerusalem: the reference 3 lines from bottom of page should read: "see Chapter IX, pp. 190/191". (see: Part II, Chapter Six).

p. 187: THE ORDER OF ST. MICHAEL OF THE WING (not: St. Michael's Wing):
for new assessment see Part III, Chapter Five /II in this volume.

p. 191: THE ORDER OF OUR LADY OF VILA VIÇOSA:
for new assessment see Part III, Chapter Five /I in this volume.
1819 in line 1 should read 1818.
Padroina do Reino in line 5 should read: *Padroeira do Reino.*

p. 196: THE ORDER OF ST. ISABEL:
for new assessment see Part III, Chapter Five /III in this volume.

p. 224: THE GRAND COLLAR OF THE THREE ORDERS:
'First Magistrate' line 1 should read: Head of State.

CHAPTER ONE

THE MOST VENERABLE ORDER OF ST. JOHN OF JERUSALEM

Sovereign Head, H.M. The Queen
Grand Prior, H.R.H. The Duke of Gloucester, GCVO
Lord Prior, Major-General The Earl Cathcart, CB, DSO, MC
Prelate: Rt. Hon. and Most Rev. The Lord Coggan
Chancellor: The Lord Grey of Naunton, GCMG, GCVO, OBE
Bailiff of Egle: The Lord Vestey, DL
Secretary General: Sir Peter Hudson, KCB, CBE, DL

As already corrected in the Errata section of this volume, the above Order, also known as the Order of St. John, is not the "Protestant Counterpart" of the Sovereign Military Order of Malta (p. 86 of *Orders of Knighthood, Awards and the Holy See*), but a British Order of Chivalry under the Crown, established by Royal Charter, open to *all* Christians as Members and, as Associates, to non-Christians also.

Her Majesty Queen Elizabeth II, wearing her robe as Sovereign of the Most Venerable Order of St. John. The Painting of Her Majesty is by Leonard Boden.

151

The Order is, like the Sovereign Military Order of Malta, a member of a small group of internationally recognised official Orders of St. John.

The original Priory of the Order was founded at Clerkenwell in ca. 1144; the buildings were burnt down during Wat Tyler's Rebellion in 1381. The Grand Prior Thomas Docwra completed the rebuilding of the great Gatehouse at Clerkenwell in 1504. In 1540 the Order was dissolved in England by Henry VIII who ordered the confiscation of all its estates and although re-established by Queen Mary in 1557, it continued to be suppressed by Queen Elizabeth I and so fell into abeyance. Eventually St. John's Gate was restored to the ownership of the British Order and its headquarters were established there through the generosity of one member of the Order in 1874. Later the original Grand Priory Church was also given back to the Order.

The Order was revived in England in 1831 through an initiative, originating from circles of the Sovereign Military Order of Malta in France, which was eventually disowned by the Grand Magistry and no official status was granted. However, the members elected to do good works and were so successful in their efforts that members of the Royal Family were, early on, attracted to support its charitable endeavours.

Two Foundations are established under the Order, St. John Ambulance, which operates worldwide, and the St. John Ophthalmic Hospital in Jerusalem.

The Grand Prior of the Most Venerable Order of St. John, H.R.H. The Duke of Gloucester, GCVO., (right), with the Lord Prior, Major-General The Earl Cathcart, CB, DSO, MC, after an investiture.

The Royal Letters Patent reconstituting the Order were signed by Queen Mary in 1557. The illuminated document (twenty-five folios) was presented to the Order in 1986. The first letter (P) is illuminated with a miniature of Queen Mary and King Philip of Spain.

In 1888 the outstanding work of the Order was rewarded with its first Royal Charter, which was granted by Queen Victoria. Since then the reigning monarch has always been the Sovereign Head of the Order, and from 1888 all Grand Priors have been members of the Royal Family.

The Order has a Prelate, sub-prelates and Chaplains. The Prelate is "a Brother of the Order of episcopal rank in the Church of England as by law established and shall be appointed by the Grand Prior to hold office during his pleasure or resignation". Being a Royal Order, the principal ecclesiastical office must be occupied by a Bishop of the Established Church. Priests and Ministers of other Christian denominations are admitted to the Chaplain's Grades of the Order, and those of episcopal rank or eminent status in the Christian Churches may be appointed by the Grand Prior to the rank of sub-Prelate of the Order. The Order has Anglican, Roman Catholic and Non-Conformist sub-Prelates and Chaplains.

In 1963 a Concordat was signed between the Most Venerable Order of St. John and the Sovereign Military Order of Malta. Many members of the Sovereign Order are also members of the Most Venerable Order. The Most

153

The Great Gatehouse, headquarters of the Order since 1144; it was burnt down during Wat Tyler's Rebellion in 1381, rebuilt by Grand Prior Thomas Dowcra in 1504. After the suppression of the Order by Queen Elizabeth I, St. John's Gate was restored to the Order in 1874.

Venerable Order is also in alliance with the Protestant Orders of northern Europe stemming from the Balley Brandenburg and the Johanniterorden.

In accordance with the laws of the Realm, the Most Venerable Order applies stringent rules to the wearing of Orders and Decorations, and the guidelines laid down by the Crown are strictly adhered to.

At religious and social functions held by the Most Venerable Order of St. John, to demonstrate the confraternal spirit of Christian Orders of Knighthood devoted to the alleviation of suffering in the world, Members of the Sovereign Military Order of Malta and those decorated with the Order *Pro Merito Melitensi* may wear their insignia or decoration of that Order. Knights of the Pontifical Equestrian Orders who have Her Majesty's unrestricted permission to wear their full insignia, may, of course, do so under the regulations of the Crown.

THE EQUESTRIAN ORDER OF THE HOLY SEPULCHRE OF JERUSALEM

I

KNIGHTS OF THE COLLAR

In 1949 Pope Pius XII instituted the rank of Knights and Dames of the Collar as the highest honour which could be bestowed on Members of the Equestrian Order of the Holy Sepulchre of Jerusalem. The number of Knights and Dames of the Collar is restricted to twelve; the Cardinal Grand Master is a Knight of the Collar *ex officio*. On 1 June 1987, the following were Knights and Dames of the Collar:

His Eminence Maximilien Cardinal de Fürstenberg, Grand Master.

His Majesty King Baudouin of the Belgians.

Her Majesty Queen Fabiola of the Belgians.

His Excellency Prince Paolo Enrico Massimo Lancellotti, Governor General.

Her Serene Highness Princess Caecilia Salm Reifferscheidt.

His Excellency Count Antonio Alberti de Poja, Vice-Governor General.

His Excellency Count Peter Metternich, Vice-Governor General.

His Excellency Dr. Russell Kendall, Vice-Governor General.

His Excellency Alfred Blasco, Vice-Governor General of Honour, Member of the Grand Magisterium.

His Excellency Douglas Jenkins, Lieutenant of Honour, Member of the Grand Magisterium.

His Excellency General Henri de Chizelle, Lieutenant of Honour.

His Excellency Dr. H. C. Hermann Abs, Lieutenant of Honour.

II

THE ORDER OF MERIT

The Order of Merit was instituted by Pope Pius XII, during the Grand Mastership of Niccolo Cardinal Canali, on 14 September 1949. At that time the Cross of Merit, which may also be conferred on non-Catholics and does not imply membership of the Order, had five classes: Knight (or Dame) Grand Collar; Knight (or Dame) Grand Cross; Knight (or Dame) Commander with Star; Knight (or Dame) Commander; Knight (or Dame).

In accordance with the revised statutes, the Order of Merit has only three classes now:

The Cross of Merit or Knight (Dame) Commander.

The Cross of Merit with Silver Star or Grand Officer.

The Cross of Merit with Gold Star or Knight (Dame) Grand Cross.

III

THE HOLY LAND PILGRIM'S CROSS

The Holy Land Pilgrim's Cross has undergone changes in name and conferment. Section III on Page 112 of *Orders of Knighthood, Awards and the Holy See* should be regarded as an historical record which is herewith updated.

The name of the Cross has been abolished and in accordance with the revised statutes of the Order of 1977, two awards for special merit have taken its place:

1.

THE PALM OF JERUSALEM
Palma di Gerusalemme

This Award is conferred in gold, silver and bronze by the Grand Master of the Order to those who have given special service to the Order or to the charitable work of the Order in the Holy Land. The decoration which is reproduced in colour in OKAHS, Plate XII/A, is worn on the left breast, hanging from a ribbon of black watered silk.

Permanent residents in the Holy Land and in special circumstances pilgrims, may receive the Award from His Beatitude the Latin Patriarch of Jerusalem and Grand Prior of the Order on behalf of the Grand Master.

2.

THE PILGRIM'S SHELL
Conchiglia del Pellegrino

The Pilgrim's Shell is reproduced in colour in OKAHS on Plate XII/A. It is awarded only to Members on a pilgrimage to Jerusalem by the Latin Patriarch of Jerusalem and Grand Prior of the Order on behalf of the Grand Master.

IV

THE UNIFORM OF KNIGHTS

The uniform is described in OKAHS p. 105. The revised statutes of the Order (1977, Titolo II, Art. V) state that the wearing of the uniform is no longer obligatory.

The photograph shows Knights wearing the tail-coat uniform, and the similarity in style with the uniforms of the Pontifical Equestrian Orders is striking.

Knights of the Equestrian Order of the Holy Sepulchre of Jerusalem in uniform.

157

V

NEW LIEUTENANCIES IN IRELAND, GIBRALTAR AND AUSTRALIA

In March 1985, a Section of the English Lieutenancy was formed in Gibraltar with founder President Augustus Victor Stagnetto, a Knight Commander of the Order. This Section was given independent status as a Magistral Delegation under the same leadership in 1987.

Another overseas Section of the English Lieutenancy was established in Perth, Western Australia, in September 1985. The founder President was Clifford Holloway, a Knight Commander of the Order. This Section will be upgraded to a National Australian Lieutenancy in April 1988.

On 26 July 1986, a Lieutenancy of the Order for All Ireland was established at the Holy Cross Abbey in County Tipperary, Ireland. The founder Lieutenant was Thomas Francis Sheahan, a Grand Officer of the Order, formerly a Member of the Lieutenancy for England and Wales.

All this new expansion of the Order was organised by His Excellency Douglas Jenkins, Knight of the Collar, as a Member of the Grand Magisterium acting under the authority of the Order's Grand Master, His Eminence Maximilien Cardinal de Fürstenberg.

VI

LIEUTENANCIES IN THE UNITED STATES OF AMERICA

There are now seven Lieutenancies in the U.S.A.:

Northern Lieutenancy:
Lieutenant: H.E. Anthony J. Adduci, Knight Commander.

North Central Lieutenancy:
Lieutenant: H.E. James E. Madigan, Knight Grand Cross.

Western Lieutenancy:
Lieutenant: H.E. John D. Boyce, Knight Commander.

Northeastern Lieutenancy:
Lieutenant: H.E. Norman A. McNeil, Knight Grand Cross.

Eastern Lieutenancy:
Lieutenant: H.E. Thomas M. Macioce, Knight Grand Cross.

Southeastern Lieutenancy:
Lieutenant: H.E. Clayton Charbonnet, Knight Commander.

Southwestern Lieutenancy:
Lieutenant: H.E. Andrew J. Layden, Grand Officer.

Both the Vice-Governor General resident in the U.S.A., His Excellency Dr. Russell Kendall, and his predecessor, Vice-Governor General of Honour His Excellency Alfred J. Blasco, are Knights of the Collar and Members of the Grand Magisterium of the Order.

Their Excellencies Vice-Governor General of Honour Alfred Blasco (left) and Vice-Governor General Dr. Russell Kendall (right).

.

CHAPTER THREE

THE NOBLE ORDER OF THE GOLDEN FLEECE
(Spanish Branch)

With regard to the constitutional changes made in 1983 to the conferment of the Order by the Grand Master, H.M. King Juan Carlos, (OKAHS p. 134, footnote), His Majesty has made further changes. 556 years after the foundation of the Order, King Juan Carlos conferred the Order on ladies for the first time.

Their Majesties Queen Beatrix of the Netherlands and Queen Margrethe II of Denmark became the first two Ladies of the Golden Fleece (Spanish Branch).

In 1983 Archbishop H. E. Cardinale said of the Spanish Golden Fleece: "It no longer possesses an aristocratic and religious character, but is more of a Royal Order with a civil character, remaining however, in the dynastic category. Nominations are made with the previous *agreement* of the Spanish Council of Ministers; it is therefore no longer subject to the exclusive authority of the Sovereign".

For the *addendum* to OKAHS the qualification "with the previous agreement" was corrected to: "the Spanish Golden Fleece is granted by the King in his capacity as Head of State, with the previous *knowledge* of the Council of Ministers".

The Royal Warrants state that His Majesty has heard the advice of the Council of Ministers before the Warrant was issued. Nevertheless, in view of several developments it would be more accurate to describe the Order as Catholic-founded rather than Catholic in character. It has long been the King's wish to confer the Order of the Golden Fleece as the premier Order of Knighthood of Spain and on similar criteria as the Order of the Garter is conferred by her Britannic Majesty.

It could previously be argued that when the Order was conferred as the gift of the Sovereign, it was 'His Most Catholic Majesty' who bestowed it. King Juan Carlos abolished this appellation in 1985, and His Majesty specifically asked for it to be removed from the caption under his portrait in OKAHS. His Majesty emphasised that he regarded this appellation as a title of honour bestowed on Spanish Monarchs over the centuries, but he did wish to stress that Parliament had decreed that the Roman Catholic Faith was no longer the official religion of Spain.

161

REAL DECRETO ..1818/.1985 concediendo el Collar de la Insigne Orden del Toisón de Oro a Su Majestad la Reina Beatrix de los Países Bajos.

Queriendo dar un relevante testimonio de mi Real - aprecio a Su Majestad la Reina Beatrix de los Países Bajos y en muestra de la tradicional amistad entre los Países - Bajos y España.

Oido el Consejo de Ministros.

Vengo en concederle el Collar de la Insigne Orden - del Toisón de Oro.

Dado en el Palacio de la Zarzuela a ..7... de Octubre de 1985.

Juan Carlos R

Felipe González Márquez

REAL DECRETO ..¹⁹⁴⁸/.¹⁹⁸⁵. por el que se concede el Collar de la Insigne Orden del Toisón de Oro a Su Majestad Margarita II, Reina de Dinamarca.

Queriendo dar un relevante testimonio de mi Real - aprecio a Su Majestad Margarita II, Reina de Dinamarca, y en muestra de la tradicional amistad entre Dinamarca y España.

Oido el Consejo de Ministros.

Vengo en concederle el Collar de la Insigne Orden - del Toisón de Oro.

Dado en el Palacio de la Zarzuela a ..²³.. de ..Octubre.. de 1985

[firma]

Felipe González Márquez

Without wishing to detract in any way from the high esteem the Order of the Golden Fleece of Spain enjoys universally, it is fair to say that the last vestige of Catholicity has disappeared. Like the Orders of the Garter and the Thistle (Great Britain) and the Order of Christ of Portugal, the Spanish Golden Fleece is now a Catholic-founded Order that has developed into a secular Order of Chivalry.

In the context of this work it is of secondary importance to pursue the argument whether the Spanish Golden Fleece is dynastic in character and the personal property of the Royal House of Bourbon of Spain, or whether it belongs to the Crown of Spain and therefore to the legitimate Head of the State of Spain. There are precedents for taking the latter view because in 1812 the national Junta of Cádiz conferred the Order of the Golden Fleece on the First Duke of Wellington and in 1870 the Cortes elected a foreign King, Amadeo of Savoy, as Grand Master during an interregnum in Spain. Another innovation set the Spanish Order apart from its Austrian counterpart: starting with Queen Isabella II, female Sovereign were allowed to assume the Sovereign Mastership of the Order.

Because of their historic importance, the Royal Warrants conferring the Golden Fleece upon the two sovereign ladies, Their Majesties Queen Beatrix of the Netherlands and Queen Margrethe II of Denmark, are reproduced here.

CHAPTER FOUR

THE SACRED AND MILITARY CONSTANTINIAN ORDER OF ST. GEORGE

The Grand Chancellor of the Order published the following list of Bailiffs Grand Cross who have been decorated with the Collar:

H.R.H. Prince Carlo of Bourbon of the Two Sicilies, Duke of Calabria, Special Representative of the Grand Master to the Order's Delegation for Christian Cultural and Social Studies.

H.R.H. Prince Antonio of Bourbon of the Two Sicilies, Grand Prefect of the Order.

H.R.H. Prince Giovanni of Bourbon of the Two Sicilies, Grand Inquisitor of the Order.

His Eminence Giuseppe Cardinal Siri, Pontifical Representative to the Order.

H.R.H. Prince Albrecht, Duke of Bavaria.

H.S.H. Prince Franz Josef, Prince of Liechtenstein.

H.M.E.H. Frà Angelo de Mojana di Cologna, Prince and Grand Master of the Sovereign Military Order of Malta.

H.R.H. Friedrich Wilhelm, Prince of Hohenzollern.

H.R.H. Prince Karl, Duke of Württemberg.

H.E. Balí Don Achille di Lorenzo, Grand Chancellor of the Order, Great Chamberlain to the Royal House of the Two Sicilies, Superintendent General of the Order's Delegation for Christian Cultural and Social Studies.

H.E. Prince Don Aspreno Giuseppe Colonna, Prince of Paliano, Principal Assistant at the Pontifical Throne; President of the Royal Deputation of the Order.

H.S.H. Karl Prince zu Schwarzenberg, Vice-President of the Royal Council of the Order.

His Royal Highness Prince Carlo, Duke of Calabria, presented on behalf of the Grand Master, the Duke of Castro, the Collar of the Sacred and Military Constantinian Order of St. George to His Eminence Giuseppee Cardinal Siri, Pontifical Representative to the Order.

H.E. Prince Don Paolo Enrico Massimo Lancellotti, Governor General of the Equestrian Order of the Holy Sepulchre; Grand Treasurer of the Order.

H.E. Don Fabio Tomacelli Filomarino, Prince of Boiano; Vice-President of the Royal Council of the Order.

H.R.H. Prince Vittorio Emanuele, Prince of Naples, Duke of Savoy.

H.E. Don Carlo Cito Filomarino, Prince of Rocca d'Aspro; Member of the Royal Deputation of the Order.

H.E. Count Andrzej Ciechanowiecki, Principal Delegate for Europe of the Order's Delegation for Christian Cultural and Social Studies; Royal Delegate of the Order for Great Britain, Ireland and Polish Affairs.

O Pacto de Paris

Bases do acordo firmado entre os Representantes de Sua Magestade El Rei o Senhor D. Manuel II, e de Sua Alteza Real o Senhor D. Duarte Nuno

declaram

O primeiro signatario a que o Seu Augusto Mandante, na falta de herdeiro directo aceitará o Successor indicado pelas Côrtes Geraes da Nação Portugueza.

b) Egualmente aceitará as resoluções das mesmas Côrtes quanto à Constituição Politica da Monarchia Restaurada

c) Que de acordo com a Santa Sé será resolvida a questão religiosa, mediante diploma a ser submettido às Côrtes.

Pelo segundo signatario foi dito que perante as declarações anteriores, o Seu Augusto Mandante pedia e recommendava a todos os seus partidarios que acatem como Rei de Portugal o Senhor Dom Manuel II, o que se unam igualmente sob a mesma bandeira que abriga todos os Monarchicos, que é a Bandeira da Patria e a Bandeira que há de salvar Portugal.

Feito em Paris, aos 17 de abril de 1922.

a) Ayres d'Ornellas
b) Conde d'Almeida e Avranches.

S. M. El Rei D MANUEL II

S.A.R. D DUARTE NUNO

In 1922 His Majesty King D. Manuel II and His Royal Highness Dom Duarte Nuno signed the Pact of Paris in which the King acknowledged that the successor to the lineage of King D. Miguel I would become the head of the Royal House of Braganza of Portugal if he should die without issue.

H.R.H. Dom Duarte Nuno, Duke of Braganza, wearing the insignia of the Order of the Golden Fleece, the Collar and Star of the Order of the Most Holy Annunciation, the Order of the Conception of Our Lady of Vila Viçosa, the Grand Cross of the Pontifical Equestrian Order of Pius IX, and the Bailiff Grand Cross of Honour and Devotion of the Sovereign Military Order of Malta.

THE ROYAL HOUSE OF BRAGANZA OF PORTUGAL

In November 1986 I received a document, the translation of which was verified in March 1987 as "a correct translation of the original declaration signed and sealed on 27 October 1986 in Lisbon by His Royal Highness Dom Duarte Pio João Miguel Henrique Pedro Gabriel Rafael, Duke of Braganza":

"I Dom Duarte, Duke of Braganza, by the Grace of God Head of the Portuguese Royal House, see fit to declare that the following Dynastic Orders belong to my House:

* Order of the Conception of
  Our Lady of Vila Viçosa.

* Order of Saint Isabel.

* Order of St. Michael of the Wing.

Each of these Dynastic Orders is self-governing by its own rules.

In order that it should be known and appropriately recorded, I have ordered this document to be drawn up signed by myself and sealed with the seal of my arms.

(signed)
Dom Duarte
Duke of Braganza"

A document from the authorities confirmed that none of the three above-mentioned Orders were on the list of Orders bestowed by the Republic of Portugal.

H.R.H. Dom Duarte, Duke of Braganza, resides in Portugal and he is universally accepted as the legitimate Head of the Royal House of Braganza.

The complex history of the Royal House of Braganza is probably the most complicated of all the royal dynasties, and as far as the genealogical intricacies of the House of Braganza are concerned, I prefer historians to fill in the sometimes unconventional details.

H.R.H. Dom Duarte, Duke of Braganza, inherited the position of Grand Master of the Orders when he became the legitimate successor to the last reigning Sovereign, although no Portuguese monarch had bestowed the

Order of St. Michael of the Wing since Dom Miguel I had died in 1866.

Because of the invasion of Portugal by Napoleon in 1807, the entire Portuguese Royal Family was forced to go to Brazil where they lived from 1808 to 1821. King John VI having returned to Portugal with his younger son Dom Miguel, he left his eldest son Dom Pedro as Regent in Brazil. In 1822, Dom Pedro severed all ties with Portugal and declared himself Emperor of Brazil, effectively deposing his own father, King John VI, who had been King of Portugal and Brazil.

The death of King John VI in 1826 led to a crisis of succession which eventually brought civil war to Portugal. The Regency Council which governed the country during the last illness of Dom John VI, recognised Dom Pedro as successor; however, Dom Pedro immediately abdicated as King of Portugal in favour of his infant daughter Dona Maria da Glória whom he married by proxy at the age of seven to her uncle, his brother Dom Miguel, believing that this would solve the crisis of succession. Dom Miguel, who was already Regent of the Realm, repudiated the marriage, and when he arrived in Lisbon in 1828, the Three Estates, Church, nobility and people, acclaimed him King, according to tradition; he reigned as Dom Miguel I, the lawfully elected King.

1828 is the first date in my assessment of the House of Braganza. Dom Miguel's policies, personal attitudes and his reign as King were traditional, he was loyal to the Holy See and the Holy Roman Church, and totally opposed to the liberalism and modernism of his brother Dom Pedro, the Emperor of Brazil. He invited the Society of Jesus, which had been expelled by his predecessors, to return to Portugal, and he re-constituted the Order of St. Michael of the Wing which soon became a most powerful political movement in the King's fight against liberalism, modernism and other enemies of the Holy Roman Church.

By 1831, Dom Pedro had become so unpopular in Brazil, facing mass demonstrations against him, that he abdicated as Emperor in favour of his infant son Pedro, and left Brazil with his daughter Dona Maria da Glória, joining other liberal émigrés who had fled Portugal for England, France and other European countries, and became their leader. He organised the overthrow of his brother Dom Miguel I, and in 1832 he sailed with fifty chartered ships and seven thousand five hundred mercenaries to Terceira in the Azores from where he launched a surprise attack on Oporto and further offensives. In 1834, King Dom Miguel I was forced to sign a peace treaty and Dom Pedro immediately declared his daughter Dona Maria da Glória of age and placed her on the throne of Portugal as Queen Maria II. Dom Pedro died in September 1834.

Dom Miguel I went into exile but first paid a visit to the Supreme Pontiff,

His Royal Highness Dom Duarte Pio João Miguel Henrique Pedro Gabriel Rafael, Duke of Braganza, Head of the Royal House of Braganza of Portugal, in audience with His Holiness Pope John Paul II in Rome. Dom Duarte Pio welcomed Pope John Paul II during the Supreme Pontiff's visit to the shrine of Our Lady of Vila Viçosa.

Gregory XVI, in Rome. Dom Miguel's marriage to Dona Maria da Glória was declared null and void by the Patriarch of Lisbon on 1 December 1834 and it is rather strange that her second betrothal, this time to Prince Auguste de Beauharnais, had already taken place by proxy in Munich on 5 November 1834. Her second husband died on 28 March 1835, two months after another betrothal in Lisbon.

Dona Maria da Glória married once more, and her third husband, Prince Ferdinand of Saxe-Coburg, was declared King Consort and after the Queen's death Regent while their son Dom Pedro was under age. Dom Pedro succeeded his mother to the throne as King Dom Pedro V in 1853 but died in 1861. His younger brother Dom Luis succeeded him and reigned until 1889. Dom Luis's son, Dom Carlos I, was declared King after his father's death, but he and his eldest son were assassinated in 1908. His second son Dom Manuel, succeeded as King Dom Manuel II; however, his reign was short-lived because the Revolution of 1910 brought his reign and the Monarchy in Portugal to an end.

In exile King Dom Miguel I still commanded wide support; his absence from Portugal did not settle the fundamental differences between the liberals and modernists on the one side and Dom Miguel's loyal supporters on the other. It was the Order of St. Michael of the Wing which organised the fight against liberalism and modernism in Portugal. Their acknowledged Grand Master was in exile, and Queen Dona Maria II and her successors in direct line were unable to exercise any control over the Order of St. Michael of the Wing which as a 'secret society' continued to support King Dom Miguel I.

171

Dom Miguel I was succeeded on his death in 1866 by his only son H.R.H. Dom Miguel (II).

King Manuel II went into exile in 1910 to England, and a meeting between him and Dom Miguel II took place in Dover in 1912. A tentative agreement with regard to the succession to the Headship of the Royal House of Braganza was discussed in case Dom Manuel should die without issue, though Dom Manuel II had not as yet married.

An important date for the Dynasty of Braganza was 12 April 1922. It was now certain that King Manuel II would have no issue, and his representative and the representative of Dom Duarte Nuno, son of D. Miguel, in whose favour Dom Miguel II had abdicated his rights on 31 July 1920, prepared and signed the Pact of Paris. The pact formed the basis for the succession to the Headship of the Royal House of Braganza.

"It has been declared:

A. by the first signatory (for H.M. King Dom Manuel II) that His August Head in default of a direct heir will accept the successor indicated by the general Côrtes of the Portuguese Nation.

B. Equally he (H.M. King Dom Manuel II) will accept the resolu-resolution of the same Côrtes as to the political constitution of the restored Monarchy.

C. With the agreement of the Holy See the religious question* will be resolved by means up of a diploma which is to be submitted to the Côrtes.

(* This refers to the Church property which had been confiscated under the liberal rule of the King's predecessors.)

By the second Signatory (for H.R.H. Dom Duarte Nuno) it was said before the proceeding Declaration His August Head (H.R.H. Dom Duarte Nuno) would ask and would recommend to all His supporters that they would accept as King of Portugal Dom Manuel II, and that they would unite loyally under the same Flag that shelters Monarchists. That is the Flag of the Motherland and the Flag that shall save Portugal."

H.R.H. Dom Miguel (II) died on 11 October 1927; King Dom Manuel II died in 1932 in England, and the lineage of the male descendants of Dona Maria II ended. Dom Duarte Nuno, Duke of Braganza, became the legitimate Head of the Royal House of Portugal.

In 1950, by the unanimous decision of the National Assembly of the Republic of Portugal, the successor to the Côrtes, H.R.H. Dom Duarte Nuno, Duke of Braganza and Head of the Royal House, was invited to

After H.R.H. Dom Duarte Nuno, Duke of Braganza and his family had returned from exile, he paid a visit to Rome where his son Dom Duarte Pio, the present Duke of Braganza, paid homage to his God-father, Pope Pius XII, after whom he was named. The Duke's younger son, Dom Miguel, who is now the heir presumptive, was also present at the audience.

return from exile with his family to his motherland. He had married in 1942 H.R.H. Dona Maria Francisca Princess of Brazil, a direct descendant of Dom Pedro, thus uniting the two branches of the Braganza family.

H.R.H. Dom Duarte Nuno, Duke of Braganza, died on 24 December 1976 in Lisbon. He was succeeded by his eldest son Dom Duarte Pio, as Duke of Braganza and Head of the Royal House. On 17 May 1982, by Royal Warrant, the Duke of Braganza conferred on his brother and heir presumptive H.R.H. The Infante Dom Miguel the dignity of Duke of Viseu and on his youngest brother, H.R.H. The Infante Dom Henrique de Braganza, the dignity of Duke of Coimbra.

These were the first ducal titles in Portugal, originally granted to Prince Henry the Navigator and his brother, Dom Pedro, by their father, King John I, who married Philippa of Lancaster in 1387.

The Order of the Conception of Our Lady of Vila Viçosa.

In May 1983 His Most Eminent Highness the Prince and Grand Master of the Sovereign Military Order of Malta, Frà Angelo de Mojana di Cologna, (right) paid a visit to Portugual H.R.H. Dom Duarte Pio, Duke of Braganza, (left), conferred on him the Grand Cross of the Order of the Conception of Our Lady of Vila Viçosa.

174

I

THE ORDER OF OUR LADY OF THE CONCEPTION OF VILA VIÇOSA
(Ordem de Nossa Senhora da Conceição de Vila Viçosa)

The Order was founded by Dom John VI, King of Portugal and Brazil (1816–1826) on 6 February 1818 in Brazil to honour Our Lady of the Conception. It was awarded for outstanding civil and military merit to Portuguese, Brazilian and foreign nationals.

The Badge of the Order is an nine-pointed, gold-rimmed, white enamelled star with nine clusters of gold rays between the arms of the star, and a small five-pointed mullet superimposed on the clusters of rays; the initial AM in the centre of the golden medallion stand for *Ave Maria*, the inscription in the blue enamelled surround reads *Padroeira do Reino* (Patron Saint of the Kingdom). The Badge is surmounted by a gold crown.

The riband of the Order is pale blue moiré with a narrow white stripe on either side. The Star of the Order is similar though larger than the Badge, and the Crown is set lower upon the badge, slightly covering the centre arm of the nine-pointed white enamelled star.

The Order was suppressed by the Government of the Portuguese Republic in 1910. It continued to be worn and conferred by the Head of the House of Braganza. The Order has never been abolished; in order to clarify matters H.R.H. Dom Duarte Pio; Duke of Braganza, made a public declaration in 1986 that the Order of Our Lady of the Conception of Vila Viçosa is a Catholic Dynastic Order of the Royal House of Portugal.

The Royal Chapel where the image of Our Lady of the Conception is revered was built under the patronage of the Military Order of Avis; it is the spiritual centre of Portuguese unity. It was visited by His Holiness Pope John Paul II on 15 May 1982.

Insignia of the Order, upper row; Esquire; Star of Grand Cross; Novice; lower row: Honorary Knight; Professed Knight; Honorary Dame.

II

THE ORDER OF ST. MICHAEL OF THE WING
(Ordem de S. Miguel da Ala)

The Order was instituted in 1171 by Dom Afonso I Henriques, first King of Portugal. The document of foundation of the Order was published in the Chronicle of the Cistercians; it records also the legend that King Dom Afonso Henriques founded the Order to commemorate the vision of the Archangel Michael's armed and winged arm that appeared in the sky during his victorious battle against the infidels at Santarém. The Order adopted the rule of St. Benedict, and the Abbot of the Cistercian Monastery of Alcobaça had jurisdiction over the Order.

Contrary to the information made available to Archbishop Cardinale who placed the Order among the extinct Catholic Orders, the Order of St. Michael of the Wing is fully chronicled. Details can be found in Part II of this book in Chapters Two, Three and Four because the Order was most diligently researched and served as an example in the examination of the *Bullarium Romanum.*

A list of the first twenty-three Grand Masters of the Order of St. Michael of the Wing in Portugal was published in 1672/1692 in the *Historie*

The Collar if the Order of St. Michael of the Wing.

177

Serie de' Maeftri , ò Gran Maeftri dell' Ordine di S. Michiele in Portogallo.

Numero de' Maeftri.	Anni di Chrifto.		Anni de Magiftraro
I.	1165 ò 1171	D. Alfonfo Henrico I. di Portogallo Fondatore dell' Ordine , Gran Maeftro. Refle anni	20
II.	1185	D. Sancio I. il popolatore Rè figliuolo di Alfonfo.	27
III.	1212	D. Alfonfo II. Rè figliuolo di Sancio ,	11
IV.	1223	D. Sancio II. Rè di lui figliuolo ,	23
V.	1246	D. Alfonfo III. figliuolo di D. Alfonfo II.	33
VI.	1279	D. Dionifio il Lauoratore figliuolo d'Alfonfo III.	46
VII.	1325	D, Alfonfo IV, chiamato il Brauo , figliuolo del Rè D. Dionifio.	32
VIII.	1357	D. Pietro fopranomato il Retto giudice , figliuolo del Rè D. Alfonfo IV.	10
IX.	1367	D. Ferdinando figliuolo del Rè D. Pietro .	16
X.	1383	D. Giouanni I. detto di buona memoria, già Maeftro di Auis, figliuolo Naturale del Rè D. Pietro.	50
XI.	1433	D. Odoardo figliuolo di D. Giouanni I.	5
XII.	1438	D. Alfonfo V. nominato l'Africano figliuolo del Rè Odoardo,	43
XIII.	1481	D. Giouanni II. fopranomato il Prencipe perfetto, figliuolo del Rè Alfonfo V.	14
XIV.	1495	D. Emanuele figliuolo dell'Infante D. Ferdinando , figliuolo del Rè D. Odoardo , fucceffe al di lui Cugino Rè D. Giouanni II.	26
XV.	1521	D. Giouanni III. figliuolo del Rè D. Emanuele.	35
XVI.	1557	D. Sebaftiano I. nato poftumo del Prencipe D. Giouanni figliuolo del Rè D. Giouanni III.	21
XVII.	1578	D. Henrico figliuolo del Rè D. Emanuele , fù Cardinale , indi Rè.	2
XVIII.	1580	D. Filippo II. Rè di Spagna, e Portogallo.	18
XIX.	1598	D. Filippo III. Rè di Spagna, e Portogallo.	23
XX.	1621	D. Filippo IV. Rè di Spagna , e Portogallo.	19
XXI.	1640	D. Giouanni IV. già Duca di Braganza acclamato Rè di Portogallo.	16
XXII.	1656	D. Alfonfo VI. Rè di Portogallo depofto.	11
XXIII.	1667	D. Pietro II. Regnante .	

Così

Grand Masters of the Order from the foundation until the end of the seventeenth century.

The High Commander of the Order of St. Michael of the Wing, H.R.H. The Infante Dom Miguel de Braganza Duke of Viseu.

Cronologiche dell'Origine degl'Ordini Militari e di tutte le Religioni Cavalleresche by the Abbot Bernardo Giustiniani.

The history of the Order from 1733 to 1912 is recorded and documented in *Historia da Franco — Maconaria em Portugal* by Prof. Manuel Borges Grainha. This covers the years from the reconstitution of the Order by King Dom Miguel I in 1848 to the beginning of the Portuguese Republic. Many other contemporary historical studies make also reference to the 'Secret Society of St. Michael of the Wing'. The Order was given this unfortunate appellation by its own Grand Masters in the nineteenth century; although never abolished, the Order was forced underground because it remained loyal to its Grand Master King Dom Miguel I, fought liberalism and modernism which the reigning Sovereigns embraced, and *"This Order, following the 1st article of its statutes, was essentially secret, militant and political; it had as its ultimate objective (2nd article) to uphold the Roman Catholic Apostolic Religion and the restoration of the legitimate succession: One of its political methods of action was to resort to arms in extraordinary events (4th article). The Grand Mastership of the Order was incumbant in the Kings of these realms (28th article) and belonged by right to King Dom Miguel I and, after him, to his legitimate successors to the Portuguese Crown"*.

In 1981 H.R.H. Dom Duarte Pio, Duke of Braganza, the legitimate successor to King Dom Miguel I, reconstituted the Order of St. Michael of the Wing as a Catholic Dynastic Order of the Royal House of Portugal. In 1987, he appointed his younger brother Dom Miguel, the Duke of Viseu, High Commander of the Order.

The Badge of the Order is a red enamelled, gold-rimmed *Long Cross Fitchy*, the lower point between two gold fleurs-de-lis, the upper point

179

ending with an inverted heart, and the points left and tight ending in a fleur-de-lis; in the centre of the Cross is a medallion in gold of the sun in splendour with sixteen rays on which is superimposed an inverted red enamelled wing; the Cross is surmounted by a white enamelled scroll with the inscription *Quis ut Deus*, pending from a gold crown. The ribbon of the Order has three equal stripes of blue, red and blue.

III

THE ORDER OF ST. ISABEL
(*Real Ordem de Santa Isabel*)

The Order was established in 1801 by the Prince Regent Dom John, the future King of Portugal Dom John VI, inspired by his wife Princess Carlota Joaquina of Spain, as an award to Catholic ladies of noble birth for deeds of charity. The Order was awarded in one class and was limited to twenty-six members under the Grand Mastership of the Queen.

The obverse of the insigna is an oval enamelled medallion portraying St. Isabel helping the poor. The medallion is surrounded by a green enamelled laurel wreath set in a gold garland of roses surmounted by a gold-winged angel. The Badge is surmounted by a gold crown. The inscription on a blue enamelled scroll reads *Pauperum Solatio* (Comfort of the Poor).

The reverse of the Badge is a white enamelled medallion with the Queen's initials CJ intertwined, surmounted by a small laurel wreath. The medallion is surrounded by a blue circlet with the inscription *Real Ordem de Santa Isabel*. On a scroll is the date of foundation 1801. The Order is worn on a pink riband tied in a bow with four narrow white stripes.

The Order was suppressed by the Government of the Portuguese Republic in 1910.

The Badge of the Order of St. Isabel.

PART IV

Part IV deals with two Orders which are neither Catholic nor Orders of Knighthood. They are of interest because the Order of Orthodox Hospitallers their Badge of Religion which is conferred on non-Orthodox as well as on Orthodox, has been received by several high Roman Catholic dignitaries and laymen. Having been instituted by a ruling Head of State who was also Head of the Orthodox Church in the country of foundation, His Beatitude Archbishop and President Makarios III of the Republic of Cyprus, but designated not to be an Order of the State of Cyprus, it is unique among all the known Orders of any kind. The insignia legitimately qualify under the prerequisits of International Law to be recognised as 'decorations'. However, both the concept of Orders of Knighthood and of 'decorations' are alien to Orthodox practice. The Badge of a Companion is therefore awarded as a Badge of Religion.

The Lambeth Cross and the Order of St. Augustine of Canterbury were founded by an Archbishop of Canterbury, the spiritual Head of the Church of England and *primus inter pares* among the Heads of the Churches in the Anglican Communion, the temporal Head of which is the British Sovereign. However, neither the Lambeth Cross nor the Order of St. Augustine of Canterbury has a Royal Charter. Their position in the national and international forum of 'Orders of Merit' is not clear.

Because of the ecumenical work between the Roman Catholic Church and the two major Christian Churches, the Orthodox Churches and the Anglican Communion, especially the Church of England, the Badges of Religion of the Orthodox Hospitallers and the Awards of Merit of the Archbishop of Canterbury are relevant addenda to *Orders of Knighthood, Awards and the Holy See.*

Top left: His Beatitude Archbishop Makarios III, President of Cyprus, first Grand Master and Temporal Protector of the Order of Orthodox Hospitallers, with the Order's Grand Chancellor, Br. Sergei Baron von Bennigsen. Top right: His Excellency the President of Cyprus, Mr. Spyros Kyprianou, with the Grand Chancellor. Below: In 1986 Baron von Bennigsen presented the insignia of a Companion with Star to the newly appointed Apostolic Nuncio in London, His Excellency Archbishop Luigi Barbarito (second from left); other recipients of a Companionship with Star were on this occasion: the Right Reverend and Right Honourable The Lord Coggan, former Archbishop of Canterbury; the Reverend Fr. Vladimir Felzmann, Chaplain to the Papal Knights in Great Britain, and Sir Sigmund Sternberg, K.C.S.G.

CHAPTER ONE

ORDERS AND THE ORTHODOX CHURCH

The Order of the Orthodox Hospitallers

Matters relating to Orders of the Orthodox Church or autocephalous Patriarchs of the Orthodox Church do not fall within the sphere of interest of the Holy See.

No reference to them would have appeared here had the late Archbishop Cardinale not considered it important to draw attention to the growing number of self-styled orders which use the appellation *Orthodox* and claim, without justification, recognition by, and sometimes union with, the Roman Catholic Church. In Chapter XI of *Orders of Knighthood, Awards and the Holy See*, page 236, the position is made absolutely clear, and the section was retained in the revised edition because the situation has not changed.

Because of the unique religious and secular status of the Order of Orthodox Hospitallers, which makes it an anomaly among all Orders, religious, chivalric, secular, the presentation differs from that of other Orders which can be found in *Orders of Knighthood, Awards and the Holy See* or in this Supplement. Parts are extracted from the certified documents and sworn affidavits; conclusions have also been based on verbal evidence and consultations with international jurists.

Only Archbishop Makarios could give the answer to the question whether it was his intention to institute an Order which was to possess and enjoy, even after his death, the privileges and rights of a State-founded Order though its real character was that of a Religious Order, or whether His Beatitude founded the Order of the Orthodox Hospitallers in the firm believe that the religious power of the Grand Master and the secular power of the Temporal Protector would for ever remain in one person? Archbishop Makarious died in 1977; the Order of the Orthodox Hospitallers has survived him and flourishes.

THE ORDER OF THE ORTHODOX HOSPITALLERS

1) The Order was founded in December 1972 as a Religious Order by His Beatitude Makarios III, Archbishop of, and Ethnarch in, Cyprus, first President of the Republic of Cyprus.

2) The Order was not founded as a chivalric Order, which is an alien concept in Orthodox theology.

3) Archbishop and President Makarios decreed that the Grandmastership of the Order should always be vested in the Archbishop of, and Ethnarch in, Cyprus, and the office of Temporal Protector in the President of the Republic of Cyprus.

4) As the spiritual Head of the Church in Cyprus and the Head of State of the Republic of Cyprus, Archbishop Makarios assumed both the office of Grand Master and Temporal Protector of the Order of the Orthodox Hospitallers.

5) Archbishop and President Makarios domiciled the Order of the Orthodox Hospitallers in the Monastery of St. Barnabas, Famagousta, in the Republic of Cyprus, and the Order has retained its Seat there with the permission of the Turkish authorities after the occupation of the Monastery by Turkey during the civil war in 1974.

6) Only members of the Orthodox faith can be members of the Order of the Orthodox Hospitallers.

7) Archbishop and President Makarios instituted a Badge of Religion which may be conferred on non-Orthodox persons for services rendered to the Order.

8) The Badge of Religion is conferred in three classes: Companion, Companion First Class and Companion with Star, and very rarely with Cordon. Companionships do not imply membership of the Order of the Orthodox Hospitallers.

9) Archbishop President Makarios decreed that the Apostolic Pro-Nuncios to Cyprus and to Great Britain, the Vicar General of the Latin Patriarch of Jerusalem in Cyprus, and the Anglican Bishop of Cyprus and the Gulf should be offered the Badge of Religion with Star on their appointment. Archbishop President Makarios also suggested that other religious leaders and public figures, especially in countries with large Orthodox communities, should be honoured with a Companionship to further good inter-denominational and inter-faiths relations.

10) To be a pan-Orthodox Order and able to operate outside Cyprus, the Order of the Orthodox Hospitallers obtained canonical regognition from the Representatives of other autocephalous Patriarchs, including the Constantinople and Moscow Patriarchates. The Patriarchs of Alexandria, Nicholas VI, and Diodros I of Jerusalem, became High Spiritual Protectors of the Order within their Canonical Territories, a

The Badges of Religion of the Orthodox Hospitallers, (left) the white-enamelled Cross *botonnée* of the Members of the Order, (centre) the Badge of a Companion 1st class, (right) the insignia of a Companion with Star.

right which can be claimed by all Metropolitans within the territory of their jurisdiction.

11) The appointment of Br. Serge Baron von Bennigsen, O.H., as Grand Chancellor and *Megas Domesticos* of the Order of the Orthodox Hospitallers by His Beatitude Archbishop Makarios was confirmed by his successors, the new Archbishop of Cyprus and the newly elected President of Cyprus.

12) Archbishop Makarios III was not only the Head of the Orthodox Church in Cyprus but also the democratically elected (and twice re-elected) President of the Republic of Cyprus; therefore Order of the Orthodox Hospitallers is in every respect a legitimate Order which is endowed with all the privileges of an Order instituted by a Head of State. The fact that it is a Religious Order has no bearing on its status in International Law.

13) The Badges of Religion and the Companionships conferred by the Order of the Orthodox Hospitallers have therefore the same legal standing in International Law as have other decorations conferred by a legitimately instituted Order.

14) The Badge of the Order of the Orthodox Hospitallers is a white enamelled, gold-rimmed, Cross *botonnée*, worn as a neck badge and also on the left breast.

15) The Badge of Religion which is conferred with a Companionship is

185

a red enamelled round medallion with a white Cross *botonnée* in the centre, and in the white surround in gold the letters: FOR THE GLORY OF GOD AND THE GOOD OF MANKIND.

16) Companions and Companions First Class wear the badge from a red ribbon, the latter with a red rosette on the ribbon, on their left breast. Companions with Star wear a seven-pointed gilded star with the enamelled badge in the centre. Companions with star and Cordon wear a red moiré sash, eight centimetres wide, over their right shoulder.

17) The Order is outside the sphere of interest of the Holy See because it is not a Catholic-founded Order, and it does not need the Holy See's approval for its existence. It is a matter of personal choice as far as Roman Catholic prelates and laymen are concerned to accept the honour of a Companion of the Order in the spirit of ecumenical collaboration between the Holy Roman Church and the Orthodox Churches.

The Order of St. Augustine of Canterbury.

RELIGIOUS AWARDS INSTITUTED BY THE SPIRITUAL HEAD OF A CHURCH OF WHICH THE SOVEREIGN IS THE TEMPORAL HEAD

THE LAMBETH CROSS
AND
THE ORDER OF ST. AUGUSTINE OF CANTERBURY

These are Awards of Merit are unique because they were instituted by the spiritual Head of a Church of which the Sovereign is the temporal Head. However, the Sovereign took no part in the Awards' institution, and is not concerned with the conferment, but because the Sovereign is the temporal Head of the Church of England as established by Law, the Awards are accorded privileges which are denied to other religious decorations.

Should, however, the Church of England one day follow other Churches in the Anglican Communion and disestablish itself or should the Sovereign resign the position of temporal Head of the Church, the position of the Order of St. Augustine of Canterbury could change.

The Lambeth Cross is restricted to those in episcopal orders, and it is both in character and appearance a pectoral cross; therefore its rôle and position would not be affected by any changes in the structure of the Church.

Because the Order of St. Augustine 1st Class — the Cross in gold — was only given to Bishops, it ceased to be conferred in 1981, and the Lambeth Cross has taken its place.

There is another difference in the conferment of the two Awards: the Lambeth Cross is given by the Archbishop of Canterbury in his capacity as Primate of All England and not as *primus inter pares* among the Metropolitans of the Anglican Communion. It is always presented by the Archbishop of Canterbury in person, and no Protocol is given with it. The Order of St. Augustine of Canterbury is awarded with a Protocol (or Letters Patent). The Archbishop of Canterbury signs the document in all his capacities; the original proposal by the Church of England Council on Foreign Affairs had strongly recommended that this Order should, like the Lambeth Cross, be conferred by the Archbishop of Canterbury as such and not as the senior Metropolitan of the Anglican Communion ". . . because we have come to the conclusion that the second alternative might lead to complications, and perhaps even to demands for participation, from outside Churches in communion with Canterbury".

This proposal was not adopted because the Archbishop of Canterbury was quite correctly advised elsewhere that the sole right of conferment was vested in him, and that the question of demanding 'participation' simply could not arise.

The international status of the Order of St. Augustine of Canterbury has never been tested, nor for that matter, has the Order's status been clarified in England. The Chancery of Orders of Knighthood in the British Realm 'took note' of the Order's foundation but made it clear that the Order as such was outside its province. It is therefore not listed among the British Orders and Decorations; however, it may be worn in the presence of the Sovereign, which suggests that the Sovereign has given tacit consent.

1.

THE LAMBETH CROSS

The Lambeth Cross was instituted by Archbishop Lang of Canterbury, who in November 1939 appointed a committee to design the decoration. The Cross was for the first time awarded on 16 June 1942, when Archbishop Lang bestowed it on the Greek Orthodox Metropolitan Archbishop Germanos of Thyateira.

The reason outlining a need for the foundation of the Lambeth Cross was prepared by a commission under Archbishop Lord Lang of Lambeth, who had retired as Archbishop of Canterbury, and submitted by the Church of England Council of Foreign Relations to the Archbishop of Canterbury *pro tempore* in 1944.

It was the wish of the spiritual Head of the Church of England to have a decoration to bestow on Prelates of the Orthodox Churches and other Christian Churches in Europe as a visible token of appreciation and gratitude, and especially as a reciprocal Award where members of the Anglican Church who had served on Delegations to Orthodox Churches in the cause of promoting mutual understanding and fellowship, had received decorations from civil governments of the countries visited.

The Lambeth Cross is awarded to Prelates who have rendered exceptional services to the cause of Christian unity and specially to strengthen the relations between these Churches and the Anglican Communion.

There have been thirty conferments of the Lambeth Cross from 1942 to 1987, the last Cross having been conferred in 1983.

Four awards of the Lambeth Cross have been made to Roman Catholic

Prelates: on 24 March 1966 to His Eminence Augustin Card. Bea of the Roman Curia; on 12 May 1967 to His Eminence Leo Joseph Card. Suenens, Primate of the Church in Belgium; on 4 October 1972 to His Eminence Johannes Card. Willebrands, President of the Pontifical Secretariat for Christian unity, Città del Vaticano; and on 1 September 1981 to the Right Reverend Alan Charles Clark, Bishop of East Anglia, England. The latter has been the only recipient in the United Kingdom.

The Lambeth Cross is gold, and the design is based on an English romanesque ivory pectoral cross of the 11th century. The figure of the Crucified Christ was adapted from a life-sized stone rood on the outside of Langford Church in Oxfordshire, which dates from about the same period. The rood at Langford has lost its head, and the head on the Lambeth Cross was adapted from contemporary Spanish romanesque crucifixes which, like the rood at Langford, are closely related to the crucifix at Lucca known as the *Volto Canto*. The inscription on the Cross says: *Hoc signum amicitiae et benedictionis D.D. Archiepiscopus Cantuariensis*. The Lambeth Cross is worn, like a pectoral cross, on a gold chain.

2.

THE ORDER OF ST. AUGUSTINE OF CANTERBURY

The Order of St. Augustine of Canterbury is awarded by the Archbishop of Canterbury in his capacity as *primus inter pares* of the Metropolitans in the Anglican Communion and as Primate of All England to clergy and laymen of Christian Churches who have contributed conspicuously to advancing friendly relations with the Churches of the Anglican Communion.

The Cross of the Order is a replica of the 8th century Cross of Canterbury which is of Celtic origin. The reverse bears an engraving of the Chair of St. Augustine of Canterbury, the ancient throne in Canterbury Cathedral, in which all Archbishops of Canterbury are enthroned, and the inscription: *IN APPRECIATION FROM THE ARCHBISHOP OF CANTERBURY.*

The Order was instituted in 1964, following a recommendation by a special committee appointed by the Church of England Council on Foreign Relations and for the first time awarded in February 1965. It was instituted in three Classes, gold, silver and bronze. The first Class was reserved entirely, and the second Class with very rare exceptions, for eminent prelates and clergy. The Cross is worn by prelates and clergy as a neck badge, pending from a riband of Canterbury-blue; laymen wear the Cross on the left breast, pending from a ribbon of the same colour.

APPENDIX

The Appendix contains information which was received after 15 June 1987

I

KNIGHTS OF THE COLLAR
OF THE
PONTIFICAL EQUESTRIAN ORDERS

On 30 June 1987, the *Assessore* of the Secretariat of State, Right Rev. Mons. Giovanni Battista Re, issued the following list of new Knights of the Collar of the Pontifical Equestrian Orders:

As of 30 June 1987 no appointments have been made to the Supreme Order of Christ and the Order of the Golden Spur since the publication of the list in 1983. The last appointment to the Supreme Order of Christ having been made on 18 February 1966 when President Saragat of Italy received the insignia.

The following Heads of State have received the Pian Collar since 1983:

H.E. President Jean Claude Duvalier of Haiti, (1984).

H.E. President Karl Carstens of the Federal Republic of Germany, (1985).

H.E. President Francesco Cossiga of Italy, (1985).

H.E. President Paul Biya of the Republic of Cameroon, (1986).

On 5 July 1987 *L'Osservatore Romano* announced that on 4 July His Holiness Pope John Paul II bestowed the supreme Order of Christ on His Most Eminent Highness Frà Angelo de Mojana di Cologna, Prince and Grand Master of the Sovereign Military Order of Malta.

II

THE ORDER OF THE WHITE EAGLE
THE ORDER OF *POLONIA RESTITUTA*

The Chief of the Chancery of the President of the Republic of Poland in Exile has informed the Holy See that in accordance with the Polish Constitution of 1935, the President of the Polish Republic in Exile, His Excellency Count Edward Raczynski, Grand Master of the Catholic-founded Orders of the White Eagle and of *Polonia Restituta*, which is the legitimate successor of the Order of St. Stanislaus, retired on 8th April, 1986. His Excellency Mr. Kazimierz Sabbat has been nominated and sworn in as the new Polish President in exile.

His Excellency Count Raczynski had held the office for seven years, and it was during his presidency that the Catholic Order of the White Eagle was moved from the list of "extinct Catholic Orders' to the list of flourishing Orders after it had been established in International Law that Poland's highest chivalric honour was extant under the Grandmastership of the Polish President in Exile though suppressed in the People's Republic of Poland.

His Excellency President Sabbat, Grand Master *pro tempore* of the Order of the White Eagle, will also continue to confer the Order of *Polonia Restituta* (the legitimate successor of the Catholic-founded Order of St. Stanislaus). The First Secretary of the Central Committee of the Communist Party of Poland confers the Order under the constitution of 1944 as a secular Order.

The practice of an Order having two legitimate grantors has precedence in International Law.

INDEX